Christmas 19

A book to pass the time during
your coming recuperation, and
to enjoy to the full when you
are once again fit enough to
enjoy a country walk!

    With love from Simon, Liz
    and the children.

The Wye Valley

overleaf: *Symonds Yat: the Wye from Yat Rock*

The Wye Valley

From River Mouth to Hereford

EDMUND J. MASON

Illustrated by
JOHN WILFORD

Robert Hale Limited
Clerkenwell House
Clerkenwell Green
London EC1R 0HT

British Library Cataloguing in Publication Data

Mason, Edmund J.
   The Wye Valley: from river mouth to Hereford.
   1. Wye, River, Valley (Wales and England)—
   Description and travel
   I. Title
   914.29'504858   DA670.W97

   ISBN 0-7090-2964-0

Photoset in Baskerville by
Rowland Phototypesetting Limited, Bury St Edmunds, Suffolk
Printed in Great Britain by
St Edmundsbury Press Limited, Bury St Edmunds, Suffolk
and bound by WBC Bookbinders

Contents

By the same author

Portrait of the Brecon Beacons
The Mendips (with A. W. Coysh and V. Waite)
Caves and Caving in Britain
Avon Villages (with Dorrien Mason)

Illustrations

Maps

Based upon the Ordnance Survey map with the permission of the controller of Her Majesty's Stationery Office. Crown Copyright Reserved.

Acknowledgements

The author wishes to record his thanks to the many people who have supplied information for use in this book, with particular thanks to the following: Mr Matthew Allen, Mrs K. Andrew, Mr and Mrs G. H. Arnold, Mr W. F. Boast, Dr Basil Cottle, Mr John Cronin, Mr Ian Dury and staff of Stuart Crystal, Messrs Lindsay and Edward Heyes, Mr Alex Jolly, Mrs M. Meredith, Mr Robin Newman, Mr O'Leary, Mr R. A. Rastell, Miss Anne Sandford, Mrs Lucas Scudamore, Mrs Russell-Steele, Mr Chris Walters, Mrs Williams, Mr and Mrs Ray Wright, Mr Jonathan Wright, the wardens and staff of the Wye Valley Warden Service, and special thanks to Mrs Dorrien Mason, for assistance with research and editing this book.

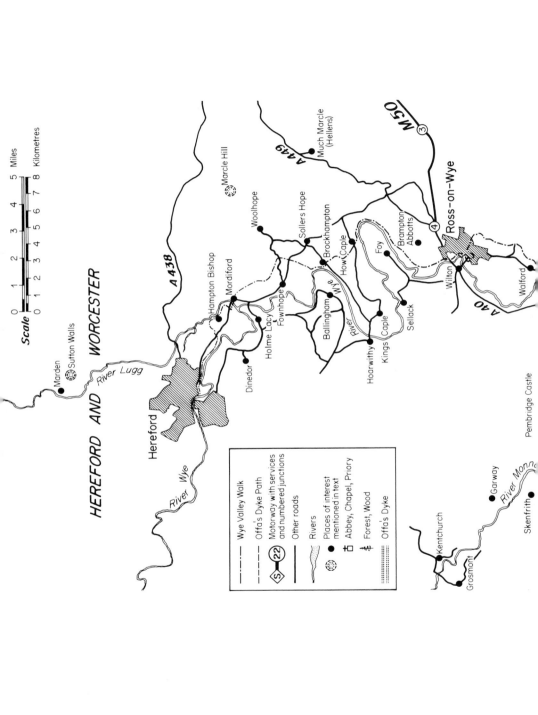

HEREFORD AND WORCESTER

Scale

Miles
0 1 2 3 4 5
0 1 2 3 4 5 6 7 8
Kilometres

Wye Valley Walk
Offa's Dyke Path
Motorway with services and numbered junctions
Other roads
Rivers
Places of interest mentioned in text
Abbey, Chapel, Priory
Forest, Wood
Offa's Dyke

Marden
Sutton Walls
River Lugg
River Wye
Hereford
A 438
Hampton Bishop
Mordiford
Holme Lacy
Dinedor
Fownhope
Ballingham
Hoarwithy
Kings Caple
Sellack
Wilton
Walford
A 40
Ross-on-Wye
Wye
River Wye
How Caple
Foy
Brampton Abbotts
Brockhampton
Sollers Hope
Woolhope
Marcle Hill
Much Marcle (Hellens)
A 449
M50
3
4
Pembridge Castle
Kentchurch
Grosmont
Garway
Skenfrith
River Monnow

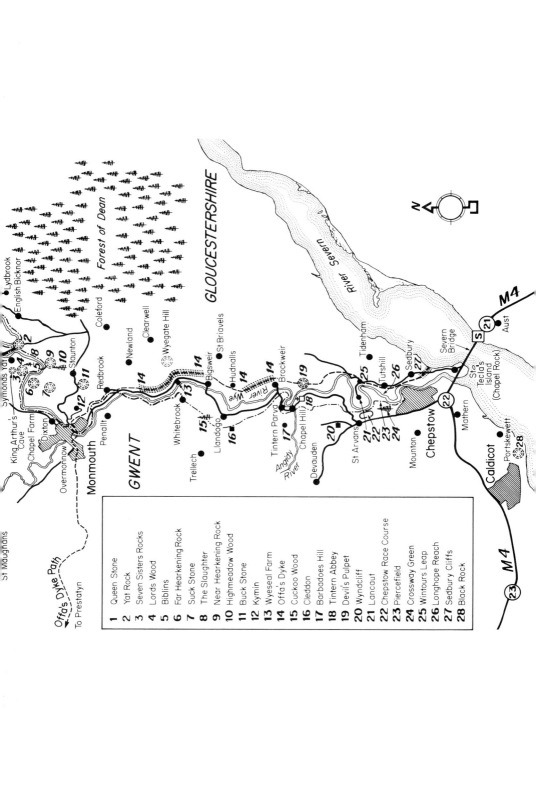

Forest of Dean

GLOUCESTERSHIRE

River Severn

M4

GWENT

Monmouth

St Maughans

Offa's Dyke Path
To Prestatyn

Lydbrook
English Bicknor
King Arthur's Cave
Chapel Farm
Symonds Yat
Dixton
Overmonnow
Penallt
Redbrook
Newland
Clearwell
Coleford
Wyegate Hill
Staunton

Trellech
Whitebrook
Llandogo
Bigsweir
St Briavels
Hudnalls
Brockweir
Tintern Parva
Chapel Hill
Devauden
St Arvans
Mounton
Chepstow
Mathern
Caldicot
Portskewett
Tidenham
Tutshill
Sedbury
Severn Bridge
St Tecla's Island (Chapel Rock)
Aust
M4

Angidy River
River Wye

N

1 Queen Stone
2 Yat Rock
3 Seven Sisters Rocks
4 Lords Wood
5 Biblins
6 Far Hearkening Rock
7 Suck Stone
8 The Slaughter
9 Near Hearkening Rock
10 Highmeadow Wood
11 Buck Stone
12 Kymin
13 Wyeseal Farm
14 Offa's Dyke
15 Cuckoo Wood
16 Cleddon
17 Barbadoes Hill
18 Tintern Abbey
19 Devil's Pulpet
20 Wyndcliff
21 Lancaut
22 Chepstow Race Course
23 Piercefield
24 Crossway Green
25 Wintours Leap
26 Longhope Reach
27 Sedbury Cliffs
28 Black Rock

———————————— 1 ————————————

Introducing the Wye Valley

How oft, in spirit have I turned to thee,
O Sylvan Wye! thou wanderer thro' the woods
How often has my spirit turned to thee!
Wordsworth

Wordsworth was certainly speaking of the Lower Wye, meander-ing through its vast woodlands and gorges, far from its source high up on the slopes of Plynlimon. The source is close to that of the Severn, but the rivers take their separate ways, not to meet again until they join to form the Bristol Channel, 130 miles to the south-east.

In its upper reaches, the Wye is essentially a Welsh river and, although it leaves the Principality at Hay, it still clings to its native land for a short distance on its western bank and in places even shares its river bed between Wales and England, before flowing through the combined English county of Hereford & Worcester. Then the Lower Wye follows and sometimes forms the boundary of the two countries, between the English Gloucester-shire and the Welsh Gwent, once the English Monmouthshire. Below Hereford, the river seems reluctant to reach the sea and wanders northwards, southwards, eastwards and westwards, in a number of loops, almost folding back on itself. Such is the double fold embracing King's Caple in the upper fold and Foy in the lower, where the river seems to be flowing in one direction on one side and in the opposite direction on the other. Symonds Yat Rock is almost completely encircled. Such meanders can be many miles round and add many miles to the length of the river.

Although the river does not always follow the Welsh boundary, it was, in ancient times, a natural barrier between the two countries, augmented by an enormous dyke, built between AD 778 and 796 by King Offa, to protect his own kingdom of Mercia. The dyke, built on the English side of the river, is sometimes a little distance from the Wye, on the higher ground for added protec-tion and views far across the river into what, in Offa's day, was potential enemy country. Today the walker can enjoy these viewpoints by taking the Offa's Dyke Path, a long-distance

Tintern Abbey

public path marked by an arrow and an acorn on directional signs.

The Offa's Dyke Path does not always follow the original course of the Dyke. It traverses undulating country, and diversions are unavoidable because of dense woodland, quarries, gradients and modern development. Although river courses are generally unchanged, man-made banks, such as Offa's Dyke, are usually mutilated by weather and by man and even by the tramping of men and animals, along the route. The contours of ancient works we see today are less formidable than they once were, as the sharp edges and scarps have flattened out, especially where the earthen banks adjoin a dry ditch. Much of the earth and stones which were dug out of the ditch to form the bank have since fallen back in, filling the ditch for about a third of its original depth, while grass, vegetation and the roots of trees have all helped destroy and soften the original contours.

However, there are still about thirteen miles of Offa's Dyke visible between Hereford and Chepstow. Some of it is quite impressive, as in the Tintern area, near the Devil's Pulpit and where it climbs the flank of Wyegate to a height of 500 feet, overlooking the bridge at Bigsweir. To walk the route of Offa's Dyke from its beginning on Sedbury Cliffs, just east of Chepstow, to Prestatyn on the North Wales coast, a distance of 168 miles, might take fourteen days at a steady pace of twelve miles a day, but much longer to include visits to the many interesting places near the route.

Another way for the walker to see the lower part of the Wye Valley is to take the Wye Valley Walk from Chepstow to Hereford, marked by directional signs of an arrow and a dot. This route, as the name suggests, is nearer the river and sometimes along its banks.

Today the Lower Wye Valley from Chepstow to Hereford is the part of the valley which most people think of as the 'Wye Valley'. It is the area covered by this book, rich in history and with a wide variation of landscape, open country, hills, woodlands and gorges, with four principal towns, Hereford, Ross, Monmouth and Chepstow, and many fascinating villages. It is one of the scenic tourist areas of Britain, and in the eighteenth and nineteenth centuries, even when it was more industrialized, it attracted many visitors. There was the 'Wye Tour', by boat then the usual means of travelling along the valley. The present valley road did not exist before 1828, and the Wye Valley railway line did not open until 1876, so that before 1828 the only direct route down the Wye was by boat – and a very pleasant and leisurely trip it must have been, except for the rowers.

Dr John Egerton, rector at Ross in 1745, used to entertain his friends by taking them down the Wye by boat, and so the idea appealed to commercially minded boatmen. The Wye Tour from Hereford to Chepstow took three days, and from Ross two days. The boats carried up to six men as rowers and ample food and drink for passengers and crew. A table occupied the centre of the boat, on which travellers could write, sketch or eat, and it was protected from sun and rain by an awning. It was usual to disembark at favourite spots for picnic lunches with tablecloths, plentiful food and wine. An overnight stop on the Ross-to-Chepstow stretch was at Monmouth at one of the hotels adjoining Agincourt Square, where there was good accommodation for the six to eight passengers.

Below Ross one favourite place to disembark for sightseeing was Symonds Yat, where after a picnic lunch, the passengers would climb to the top of Yat Rock, still a great tourist attraction for the remarkable views, and descend the other side to join the boat again. The boatmen in the meantime had navigated the five-mile loop around the rock. At Tintern, a visit was made to the abbey ruins. The Reverend William Gilpin, in describing the journey down the Wye he made in 1770, mentioned that the beggars who lived in the hovels around the abbey would offer their services as guides to the passengers disembarking at Tintern. Charles Heath, who in 1799 wrote of his own excursion down the Wye, also refers to them. They probably included some of the earlier would-be guides, although a little older. Fortunately the beggars have gone, but so have the passenger river craft at Tintern. Another port of call on nearing Chepstow was Piercefield, then a private estate but now the Chepstow racecourse.

The Wye Tour thrived during the Napoleonic Wars, when tourism within Britain enjoyed a boom period, catering for people who could no longer travel around the Continent, but once the wars were over and European travel became easier, the Wye Tour declined. However, the well-known attractions of the Wye Valley continued to bring many visitors, some of them famous. Wordsworth came on more than one occasion and wrote of its unique beauty. George Bernard Shaw, when staying in the area, wrote to Ellen Terry of the fascinations of the Wye – praise indeed from such a critic. No doubt it was he who, on a visit to Llanthony

The Market, Agincourt Square, Monmouth

The Old House, Hereford

Priory, scrawled across the Priory Hotel visitor's book in large letters 'Came to tea G.B.S.', in striking contrast to the small writing of the many visitors to the hotel. Nelson, too, came to the Wye Valley, both on duty to inspect timber in the Forest of Dean, for the Forest supplied much of the timber for British warships, and on an official visit in 1802. He referred to the Wye as 'such a little gut of a river' during a boat journey, but what else could be expected from a sailor used to the open sea and without a poet's mind? Charles Dickens, too, visited the valley, for in 1867 he met his biographer, John Forster, at the Royal Hotel in Ross.

Woodrow Wilson and many other famous people have visited, but others came to stay, such as Sir Edward Elgar, who settled in Hereford in 1894. Other celebrities have been born in the valley, even royalty, for Henry V was born at Monmouth. Nell Gwynne is said to have been born in Hereford, although there is some division of opinion about this, as some say she was born near London's Drury Lane. We may be more certain about other Hereford-born theatrical players. David Garrick was born in Hereford in 1717, and Roger Kemble, the father of Sarah Siddons, was born there, so Hereford has strong links with the

London theatre of Drury Lane. Not all the Kembles were actors. Long before the acting generation, a priest, John Kemble, was martyred on Widemarsh Common in 1679.

There is still some boating on the river and quite a lot of canoeing, often by visiting schools and local clubs, mostly on specific stretches of the river, such as at Symonds Yat, where the rapids set a challenge to experienced canoeists. Canoeing contests are sometimes held at Hereford and Symonds Yat, and it is probably fair to say that canoes are the most common craft on the river. A few pleasure-boats of the larger variety, 'juggernauts' the local owners of small boats call them, ply on the river at Symonds Yat during the summer season, but distance is limited as the depth of the river in most places is unsuitable. There are smaller boats too for small parties. The boatmen canvas for customers, and the price of the trip varies according to the number of people who can be collected to share the cost. At Chepstow, where the river is tidal, pleasure trips are sometimes arranged.

The Wye was once a commercial river, and iron, coal, timber, bark and other materials were carried by the flat-bottomed barge-like trows, built for shallow waters. The name 'trow' is derived from an Anglo-Saxon word, *trog*, meaning a trough, because of the shape. These vessels carried their cargoes down the Wye, across the Severn Estuary and up the River Avon to Bristol. They came up the river on the tide, but even a high tide does not extend beyond Llandogo, and above Llandogo progress was possible in places only by dragging by men and horses. The trows have gone with the industries they served, but there are still reminders of the trade in pub names such as 'The Severn Trow' and, in Bristol, 'The Llandoger Trow', the famous inn adjoining the quay still known as Welsh Back, where the trows used to moor when trading with Bristol.

As we see the heavily wooded Lower Wye Valley today, in all its rural splendour, it is perhaps difficult to imagine that it was ever an industrial valley, but it was inevitable, with iron, coal and timber at hand, with water-power from the fast-running tributaries and river transport, that small-scale industries would grow up in the valley. There were iron-, brass- and paperworks and shipbuilding, but most of the evidence of industry has practically disappeared, leaving a few ruins here and there, decaying wharfs and millponds behind garden hedges, not always easy to find and providing interesting hunting grounds for the industrial historian in pleasant surroundings. The woodlands still provide timber, and coal-mining on a small scale is still carried out by the free miners in the Forest of Dean which adjoins the Wye's east bank.

There is always the ancient and present occupation on the Wye, salmon fishing. The river is famous for its salmon, and problems have been created from time to time by illicit trawling and netting. Efforts to regulate salmon fishing were made from early days, and better control was introduced by the Salmon Fisheries Act of 1861, but poaching and excess netting have remained a problem. In recent years the number of salmon has declined in the Wye as in other rivers, perhaps partly due to trawling in the Channel and the breeding-grounds.

The scenic variation of the Lower Wye Valley, like that of any other region, is dependent mainly on the underlying rocks. Most of the area is Old Red Sandstone, which produces the rich red soil colour of the more open land around Hereford and on the flanks of much of the valley. When used for building, its warm tints show well in the sun, but it weathers badly and soil erosion softens the contours of the hills, so that in the Hereford area low, round-topped wooded hills and open country predominate, through which the river winds its sinuous way.

Below Fownhope the river makes two of its largest bends, encompassing several villages within its loops. It skirts Ross, citadel-like on its hill, passes Goodrich with its castle and Welsh Bicknor on another loop, and sweeps northwards nearly up to Goodrich again and then southwards to Symonds Yat.

The name 'Yat', a gateway, is appropriate, for the river enters a gorge, with cliffs and steep wooded slopes rising on both sides, comprised predominantly of hard limestones, much less prone to weather erosion than the softer Old Red Sandstone. The area is a geologist's delight, for here we have the Crease Limestone, from an old Welsh word meaning a jacket, for the rock contains voids in which haematite, iron ore, is often deposited, and some hollows on the wooded slopes show where miners once dug for the ore.

The geologist can study not only Crease Limestone but other varieties of rock, such as dolomite, quartz conglomerate and oolite. Quartz conglomerate, which produces some of the rock buffs along the gorge, is a hard sandstone and so named because it contains within its matrix numerous rounded white quartz pebbles. As a mixture, it is a conglomerate or what is commonly called a pudding stone, and because of its hardness it was the material used for millstones.

There are also softer rocks in the gorge, shales and sandstones

Goodrich Castle

which form the more gentle slopes. Because of the complexity of rocks, the gorge does not have that uniformity of character of so many gorges which cut through one type of rock. In the Symonds Yat Gorge there are precipitous rock faces and wooded slopes, and here and there above the trees of the lower slopes a detached stack rears its head. These are often known by fanciful names. At Symonds Yat the river makes a five-mile loop, almost encircling the famous view promontory Yat Rock. After passing beneath the Seven Sisters Rocks, the river takes a less winding course to Monmouth, and at Tintern it enters the limestone again, finally leaving the Old Red Sandstone. Here there is no limestone gorge, for the valley is wider and the rock bluffs of Carboniferous limestone are further apart. Trees mask the rock escarpments, but between the woodlands appear great limestone cliffs and old quarries.

Between Tintern and Chepstow the rock faces come close to the road in places and there are warning signs of falling rocks, and safety netting. The Carboniferous limestone can be a treacherous rock because of its many fissures. It has not the same safety for rock-climbers as other rocks, such as granite, and it is easy to dislodge a piece of rock on a weathered face. It offers a challenge to the expert climber, who would see that he was properly roped. Climbers can often be seen on rock faces, such as those in the vicinity of Wintour's Leap, but there have been fatal accidents, usually to inexperienced climbers.

Because of its tendency to shatter and the difficulty of working it to flat faces, it is not a suitable building stone and is fit only for rubble construction, as a core for dressed stone and for rough stone walling. It is quarried principally as road stone. There are several quarries in the area, but most have long since been abandoned and have now become indistinguishable from natural rock faces. Some quarrying is still carried on in the lower part of the valley.

As the river passes the Piercefield Estate, it runs almost straight for a mile, the longest straight stretch, Longhope Reach, on its journey from Hereford to Chepstow. Near the river bank is Otter Hole, the only extensive stalagmite cave in this area. It is accessible only to properly equipped and experienced cavers as the entrance is below the river at high tide. From Chepstow bridge can be seen the last of the limestone in the river's course before it joins the Severn.

There are no deposits left by the Ice Ages in the Wye Valley below Hereford, as this appears to have been the southern limit of glaciation. A few scattered gravels probably belong to that period, but the terminal moraines just above Hereford indicate the extent of the advance of the Wye glacier, which was fed by intrusive ice from the Welsh uplands.

Two separate rock formations in the Wye Valley are the Buckstone, a rocking stone or logan just outside Staunton and the Suckstone about a mile and a quarter to the north in High-meadow Woods.

Some stones in the Lower Wye Valley were placed in position for reasons known only to prehistoric man. At Trellech are three tall stones of quartz conglomerate, known as Harold's Stones, the only Bronze Age Alignment in our area, although there is the odd standing stone such as the Queen Stone in the field across the river from Old Forge between Whitchurch and Goodrich.

Evidence of an earlier prehistoric period was found in King Arthur's Cave, high in Lords Wood above the Seven Sisters Rocks and to a lesser extent in Merlin's Cave, not far away, on a steep slope, near Old Forge. In King Arthur's Cave were found bones of extinct animals of the Old Stone Age and evidence of occupation by men of this and later periods. The deposits in

The stable block, Piercefield

Merlin's Cave were not so rich but also produced finds from these periods.

King Arthur's Cave, the Seven Sisters Rocks, the Suckstone and the Buckstone are almost in line, a coincidence which ley-line enthusiasts may find of interest. Opposite King Arthur's Cave, on the other side of the river is the Far Hearkening Rock and near the Suckstone is the Near Hearkening Rock, so named because they are said to have been used by gamekeepers as listening posts, as it was believed that poachers could be heard with the aid of the rocks throwing back the sounds.

Here are High Meadow Woods, a hunting ground for the botanist, with a wide range of trees and ground foliage, attracting in turn a wide variety of wild life, with many birds, small animals and insects. There is still the herd of fallow deer whose chief habitat in the Forest is High Meadow Woods. The wild boar of the old royal hunting forest have long since disappeared, but descendants of the fallow deer, once hunted by King John, remained until about 1855. In 1842 some red deer were introduced but they survived for only about six years. The present fallow deer were probably visitors from elsewhere which have now made their home and breed in the area.

The great variety of landscape in the valley is reflected in the variety of plant life. The sheltered limestone slopes are rich in limestone flora, while along the banks of the Wye are found all kinds of wild grasses. There is a whole range of deciduous trees and various types of conifers. Besides the range of conifers, the Forestry Commission has introduced deciduous trees not normally found in the area, and these add a great deal to the colours in the spring and summer foliage and particularly in the autumn, when the sides of the valley are covered with a multitude of warm tints.

In the early days of the Forestry Commission it seemed as if much of the woodlands would be replaced by military-like rows of conifers with no shade of colour to distinguish one tree from another. However, this is not to be an entirely Scandinavian landscape, and the Commission have taken both conifer and native broad-leaved forests under their care, while relaxing their restrictions about public access. It now trusts visitors to keep the woodlands tidy and to be on guard against starting forest fires, and they can now walk freely through much of the Forestry Commission's land. There are picnic sites, car-parks and many marked woodland paths and trails, often leading up to heights above the valley with views of several counties.

The oakwoods are characteristics of the Forest, and in the past charcoal-burners, shipbuilders and miners have taken their toll. Timber is a valuable commodity, and grants were made by the Crown, sometimes of the whole forest, to investors who made vast sums by the sale of the oakwoods. One was Sir John Wintour, who obtained a grant from Charles I and then engaged a large army to cut down the timber. Fortunately the oakwoods were invaluable to the Navy, and after an inspection by Nelson in 1802 extensive oak planting was carried out to maintain a steady supply for shipbuilding. Some of the existing trees may well date from that period, or even earlier. The Newland Oak, which collapsed in 1955, had a girth of forty-four feet.

Although that part of the Wye Valley described in this book is mostly hills and woodland, lush fields near the river provide excellent pasture, particularly south of Hereford, and there is little arable land. It was round Hereford that the Hereford cattle with their characteristic red coats and white faces and markings were bred, and for that matter are still being bred, to produce the finest beef cattle in the world. They are sturdy cattle, able to stand up to most conditions. The Hereford was first introduced abroad

Woodland cottage, Goodrich, near Flanesford Priory

to the United States in 1816 or 1817 by Henry Clay, who acquired
a bull, a cow and a heifer for his holding in Kentucky, and in 1860
the breed arrived in Canada. The American Hereford Cattle
Breeders Association, which later became the American Hereford
Association, was formed in 1881 and, although they are now bred
in many places abroad, Herefordshire is still the main breeding
area in Britain. It was the Hereford breed which was responsible
for setting up the great cattle industry of Argentina, and no doubt
cattle whose ancestors came from Herefordshire return to Britain
as corned beef.

   In its lower reaches, south of Monmouth, the Wye is very much
a border river, and the mingling of the two cultures is reflected in
the placenames. Near the river on the Welsh side, English names
predominate, Chepstow, Monmouth, Whitebrook, but Llandogo

is a Welsh name, and as you climb the slopes up to the old road to Monmouth, the Welsh names take over, Devauden, Trellech, Pen-y-garn, Penallt. Although little or no Welsh is spoken, it is interesting to note the Welsh intonation. On the Gloucester side of the river, the place-names are English, but even here there are exceptions, such as Lancaut, by the river below Wintour's Leap, though the Welsh double 'll' has been dropped.

The Approach to the Wye

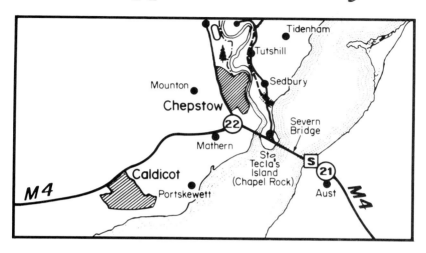

The Lower Wye Valley can be approached from many directions: from the north through Ross, from Newport from the west, via the Forest of Dean or the Gloucester road from the east by following the banks of the Severn, or by the Severn Bridge from the south.

With the motorway, the toll bridge across the Severn and the Wye has made the Wye Valley far more accessible from Bristol and London. Completed in 1966, it replaced the car ferry which plied between Aust and Beachley. As the ferry could run only according to the tides, the hours of operating were limited and at other times the traveller from Bristol or Bath was forced to travel by road to the nearest bridge at Gloucester and then back along the opposite bank, a distance of about sixty miles.

Travelling on the old car ferry was quite an experience and an exercise in patience. Cars would queue at Aust and, as the number of cars which could be carried during the several cross-ings was limited, late-comers were told that they would have to make their journey by road. It could be an hour before you were ready to board, and even then you could be told that, due to delays in loading or unloading, your chances of a crossing were slim. There was a tea-room at the ticket office, now fast falling into decay, but the driver would have to remain in the vehicle to keep

St Mary's church, Chepstow

up with the queue. The boats were large enough only for private
cars or light vans, so all heavier traffic had to go by road.

I have often waited at Aust for the *Severn King*, the *Severn Queen*
or the *Severn Princess* to loom out of the mist and tie up at the jetty.
Boarding the boat was not easy. The jetty was narrow and sloped
down to the water. You then had to turn the car sideways as the
wooden ramp, which was let down from the side of the boat like a
drawbridge, was at right angles to the jetty, its gradient depend-
ing on the height of the tide. It could take quite a bit of manoeuvr-
ing to get the car into position on the slope of the jetty, and you
had to be careful to avoid going into the water.

Several disasters had occurred in the days of the previous old
rowing-boat ferry. On one occasion the boat overturned, throwing passengers and cattle into the river. A number of passengers
were drowned, but a few made the shore by clinging to the tails of
the cattle. The victims are buried in the churchyard at Aust
adjoining the church porch. In recent years a family of three were
drowned by the rising tide when walking on a sandbank off
Beachley.

The crossing Aust to Beachley is known as 'Old Passage' and
was reputedly used by a group of Celtic bishops in AD 603 on the
way to meet St Augustine, who had come to Aust on a mission to
unite the Celtic Church with that of Rome. It is said that before
making the journey the bishops had consulted a wise man, who
advised them that, if St Augustine did not rise from his seat to
greet them, they were to take this as evidence of his pride and not
trust him. He remained seated and so the bishops went home,
back again across the Old Passage.

The crossing has been used from earliest times, as it is the
narrowest part of the Severn, and it is known as 'Old Passage' to
distinguish it from 'New Passage', two miles along the Welsh
coast at the Black Rock, near Portskewett, although it has not
been used as a crossing for many years. It was over twice the
width of the Beachley-Aust crossing, but it was possible to cross in
stages, if necessary, because of the reefs and sandbanks at low
tide.

It was on one of these, the English Stones, that sixty Parliamentarian soldiers were drowned while pursuing Charles I and
his force. On returning from ferrying the Royalists to the English
shore, the boatmen found the Parliamentarians waiting at the
Black Rock, demanding passage. They made excuses about the
tide, but the troopers insisted. The boatmen landed them on

Beachley, St Tecla's island or Chapel Rock

the English Stones, from which point the reef appears to extend to the English shore and the deep, wide, intervening channel is obscured, and then left the troopers, with all their equipment, to face the fast-rising tide. Cromwell was so angry that he closed the ferry, and it was not re-opened for a hundred years.

In the last century, New Passage was popular with horse-drawn coach travellers, and later the railway connected with it and unloaded passengers onto the ferry, but now the trains run under the Severn by a tunnel.

There is a certain beauty about the Severn Bridge when viewed from a distance, when the steelwork looks like strands of gossamer and the traffic, passing over its central hump, like toys, but I still have some yearnings for the old ferry, whose boats and crew were familiar sights. I remember the morning during the war when I arrived at Aust to await the first ferry. Suddenly an RAF plane came out of the blue, swooped low over the roof of the car and sped up the Severn. The slipstream made the wooden framework of the jetty rock and I quite expected the whole structure to collapse into the Severn.

One of my jobs was to find sites at Beachley and at Aust for labour camps in readiness for the building of the Severn Bridge. The idea of a bridge had been mooted several times but had come to nothing. One farmer said he would show me the piece of land he had offered my grandad for the same purpose, but I gave him my solemn assurance that there would be no more delays. Imagine my dismay on finding a teleprint waiting for me at the office stating that the project had been postponed once more for financial reasons. I had no heart to break the news to the farmer, so sent an assistant.

'What did he say?' I asked, when he returned.

'Oh,' he said, 'I am not surprised, but tell your boss, I will keep it for his grandson.'

As it happened, the delay was not that long, and so the great bridge designed by Sir Gilbert Roberts connecting the West of England with South Wales was opened in 1966. It was not anticipated that there would be such an increase in traffic, and the future suitability of the bridge to cope with the ever-growing traffic has been questioned. There are really two bridges, almost following, for no sooner does the road cross the Severn than it almost immediately crosses the Wye. The narrow peninsula which separates the Severn from the mouth of the Wye can be seen from the bridge, together with the little island of St Tecla, with its navigation light.

The old way to Beachley was from Aust by the ferry, but now the way is round by Sedbury, reached by going through Chepstow, over the bridge across the Wye and up the hill, with fine views of Chepstow Castle to Tutshill, where the road to Beachley turns south. A short distance along this road is an even finer view of Chepstow Castle.

Sedbury has quite a number of new houses, and just beyond the village a fingerpost on the right directs you to the Offa's Dyke Footpath, for the road cuts across the Dyke here soon after its beginning on Sedbury Cliffs. On the left is the eighteenth-century Sedbury Park (now the Sedbury Home School). In 1828 it was the birthplace of Eleanor Ormerod, a great entomologist honoured by Britain, France and Russia for her work on insects. She was consulted by many entomologists of her time and was the first woman to be awarded the LL D degree by Edinburgh University.

It has been suggested that it was at Sedbury Cliffs or nearby and not at Wintour's Leap that Sir John Wintour made his famous plunge on horseback and survived, which would have seemed unlikely from the heights of Wintour's Leap. Among his escapades as a Royalist leader, it is said that he was surprised by one Colonel Massey and his Roundheads while the Colonel was

The Severn Bridge

inspecting the cliffs at Sedbury for fortification against a Severn crossing. The survivors escaped down the cliffs to the boats. As Wintour escaped from a later surprise engagement at Lancaut, near the Leap, it is just possible that the two events may have become confused.

The road through Sedbury is a busy one (even busier when the Aust ferry ran; now the traffic bypasses Sedbury), for it serves the Army Apprentices' College, whose buildings occupy nearly the whole of the Beachley peninsula. The entrance is down the road below the Offa's Dyke path, and just within the gate, or by looking over the low wall, you can see the last muzzle-loader cannon of its type on the British mainland. It points up the Severn, but it was never fired in an engagement. Originally it occupied the old 'Well Battery' adjoining the lighthouse on Flat Holm, an island in the Bristol Channel between Weston-super-Mare and Cardiff, but it was removed to Beachley by the army apprentices in 1964. A Mark III, it was a new gun when it was installed with its companions on Flat Holm in the 1860s, but within a few years it had become obsolete because of the introduction of breeches in heavy artillery, and the only firing it ever did was in practice. Most of its companions were cut up for scrap metal (those on Flat

Holm's sister island, Steep Holm, escaped, except for an occasional cut) but they never reached the melting pot. Because of the labour involved and the reluctance of boat-owners to risk their vessels in a temperamental sea against a rocky island, the scrap merchants decided to abandon the guns. And so, with the exception of the gun at the Army Apprentices' College, they have all remained on the two islands. All others on the mainland have years since been reduced to scrap metal. The gun is seven-inch and rifled and weighs about seven tons.

The Army Apprentices' College was established at Beachley in 1924. It was then known as the Boys' Technical School and later as the Army Technical School (Boys). 'Join the Army and Learn a Trade' is a Ministry of Defence advertising slogan. They certainly do so at Beachley, for, in return for service, recruits can learn a trade from a wide range of subjects including metalwork, car-maintenance and printing. Beachley and Sedbury provide much of the accommodation for tutors, staff and others connected with the college.

With Chepstow, the peninsula has always been a strategic site. In the Civil War, both sides struggled to get possession of Chepstow Castle and the ferry at Beachley.

Because of the proximity of the Bristol Channel, shipbuilding at the mouth of the Wye was long a thriving industry. In 1917 the Government built a shipyard at Beachley as an adjunct to the already well-established shipyard at Chepstow, but no vessel was ever completed at Beachley, as the First World War came to an end. For years railway lines and hutments covered the peninsula, but today they have been obliterated by the Apprentices College. The peninsula is now a quiet place where peacetime recruits go about their work and the occasional tourist drives down the Beachley Road to look at the views across the Severn estuary. The estuary, too, is quiet, for it is beyond the channel ports downstream at Newport, Cardiff, Avonmouth and Portbury. Not even a trow, those sailing barges that carried their cargoes down the Wye, is to be seen. A few left their rotting hulks in the mud of the Severn foreshores.

Near the bottom of the Beachley Road is the Old Passage Hotel, a stopping-place for those who had braved the channel passage on the *Severn King*, *Queen* or *Princess*. Since then it has been considerably extended, with a restaurant, car- and coach-parks, and it is a residential hotel as well. Since the Beachley Road ends at the old ferry crossing, you may wonder where it gets its customers, but there is quite a population at the Army Apprentices' College and the extensive housing estates at Sedbury. People come from Chepstow and elsewhere at weekends and evenings to see the views from the car-park over Beachley Bay and the adjoining Severn Bridge. Upstream on the eastern side of the estuary can be seen the gleaming white structure of Oldbury power station and downstream from the bridge is the disused ramp at the Aust end of the old ferry.

At the bottom of the road below the hotel, which was the vicarage before it became a pub, is the stone ramp of the ferry and one of the derelict buildings adjoining it. The road bends round past the ramp, but the motorist is soon stopped by a padlocked gate. Beyond, the road becomes a track, entered by a stile. You can walk between the bank of the Severn and the perimeter fence of the college and look up at the underside of the Severn Bridge high above. The bank of grass and bushes conceals many rabbit holes, and now and then a rabbit will dash across the path. Many years ago it was suggested that the track be made into a promenade and Beachley into a second 'Brighton', with all the amenities of a seaside resort.

Further along the track is one of the two high electricity pylons which carry the cables over the estuary, and a small clearing overlooks the Wye mouth. Beyond, the track descends into the marshland adjoining the Wye.

To the left, we look down on St Tecla's Island, joined to the peninsula by a rocky and muddy reef at low tide. On this tiny island are the foundations of what is thought to have been a hermitage, and the island is sometimes known as Chapel Rock. In 1750 Ralph Allen of Bath wanted to rebuild the chapel, but the then owners refused permission. The small island is crowned by a navigation light. Perhaps there was always a beacon there, although originally it may have been only a bonfire. Hermits living on islands often made it their duty to attend to navigation lights.

Tradition has it that the saintly Tecla lived there and was murdered by a marauding band of Danes. Her name has been connected with the island since 1712, while the chapel is recorded as having been there in 1291. In 1385 it was dedicated to St Tiriocus, and at the Dissolution in 1535 it was recorded as 'St Triacus', from which the name of St Tecla was probably derived. It has been written in various ways and was interpreted by James Wood, whose manuscripts are in Newport Reference Library, as 'St Twrog'.

Caldicot Castle

Caldicot Castle is only a mile and a half along the Welsh coast from the mouth of the Wye, but to reach it we have to return to Chepstow and travel five miles south-west, on the B4245. Set in a country park with picnic places and children's play and adventure areas, the ruins date from the twelfth and fourteenth centuries. From Norman times until it became part of a farm in 1521, it was held almost continuously by members of the same family by descent, relationship or marriage. In the twelfth century, it passed by the marriage of the heiress, Margaret, daughter of Milo Fitzwalter, to Humphrey de Bohun, who was succeeded by a long line of de Bohuns. When the last of the name died a later Humphrey de Bohun, in 1373, he left two daughters as co-heiresses, Eleanor and Mary. As Eleanor was only seven and her sister three, they became wards of Edward III, and when she was sixteen, Eleanor married one of Edward's sons, Thomas of Woodstock, who carried out improvements to the castle.

In the reign of his nephew Richard II, Thomas was arrested and disappeared, presumably murdered on the orders of the King. He left a daughter, Anne, who married Edmund, Earl of Stafford. Eleanor's sister, the co-heiress Mary, had married John of Gaunt's son, Henry of Bolingbroke, who later became Henry IV, and until 1521 the castle was held by descendants and kinsmen of the two heiresses of the last Humphrey de Bohun. After 1521 it ceased to be occupied as a castle. Today it is the property of the Chepstow Rural District Council, who have done much to restore it to its present condition.

Most of the castle is in ruins, but some restoration was carried out in the nineteenth century, and parts serviceable today include one of the towers, used for exhibitions, and the large building adjoining the main entrance, which incorporates what is known as the Great Hall, now used for Caldicot's medieval banquets.

Some years ago, I decided to sample the banquet. As I passed through the great gate of the castle, a young man approached me and said, 'Excuse me, sir, but would you be the baron this evening?'

'I've never been a baron,' I replied. 'What do I do?'

'You make the opening speech and propose a loyal toast and sit at the high table.'

It sounded interesting and so I agreed.

My wife and I were asked to remain in an ante-chamber where a minstrel, seated in a window recess, was strumming out some medieval tunes. Presently in walked a brilliant procession of countesses, ladies-in-waiting and pages headed by a herald. We were placed behind the herald and walked regally round the banquet hall to be conducted to our thrones.

After making my welcoming speech, I was asked to 'break bread', which was then distributed to the other guests. Each guest had been served with a platter and a dagger-like knife, for we were expected to eat with our fingers in medieval fashion. A finger-bowl of rosewater was at the side of each place – an American gentleman seated nearby drank his rosewater; I don't suppose it did him any harm. As the baron, I was served first, but not until the food-taster had sampled it in case of poison.

At the end of the meal, I proposed the loyal toast, not forgetting the Prince of Wales as we were in his Principality. Then we had the musical entertainment which lasted late into the evening.

To the north of Caldicot and 2½ miles south-west of Chepstow is Mathern, with its parish church of St Tewdric, commemorated by a tablet on the chancel wall, erected by Bishop Godwin of Llandaff, who resided in Mathern in the early seventeenth century. It bears the following inscription from the Book of Llandaff of about 1200:

> Here lyeth intombed the body of Theoderick, King of Morganuck, or Glamorgan, commonly called St Thewdrick, and accounted a martyr because he was slain in a battle against the Saxons, being then pagans, and in defence of the Christian religion. The battle was fought at Tintern, where he obtained a great victory. He died here, being on his way homeward, three days after the battle, having taken order with Maurice, his son who succeeded him in his kingdom, that in the same place he should happen to discease, a Church should be built and his body buried in ye same, which was accordingly performed in the year 600.

A stone coffin containing a skeleton was found under the floor beneath the tablet in 1881, when the chancel was being repaired. Although the date on the tablet is 600, some argue that the event took place about 475. The ancient name for Mathern was Mertyr Teudiric, 'Merthyr' being the modern Welsh name for 'martyr'. The church is certainly of early foundation, and although now mainly of thirteenth-century work, it contains traces of earlier work, possibly even Saxon. The tower was built in 1480 in the Perpendicular style of the times, resembling the architecturally famous church towers of the same period of Somerset. It is a three-stage tower with castellated parapet.

It is not often that four bishops are buried in a parish church, but Mathern was once the seat of the bishops of Llandaff, who had their palace nearby, moving to Mathern when the Llandaff palace was destroyed during the Glyndwr uprisings about 1403. Mathern remained the principal residence of the bishops for about 300 years. Although their graves are not marked, four bishops, Salley, Kitchin, Jones and Blethin, all of the sixteenth century, were probably buried in front of the altar. Near the church is the old Bishops' Palace. It has been rebuilt and altered from time to time and is now occupied by private residents.

In the churchyard, a flat stone, a short distance from the south door, marks the grave of John Lee, who died in 1825 at the grand old age of 103. His epitaph reads:

> John Lee is dead, that good old man,
> We ne'er shall see him more;
> He used to wear an old drab coat
> All buttoned down before.

The reference to the buttoned coat, however, is not unique to Mathern.

To the north and west of Chepstow is Mounton, a place not of past ecclesiastical interest, like Mathern, but of past industry, for here carpets, cloth and paper were once made in the mills which bordered the Mounton brook. Mills flourished here from the latter half of the sixteenth century and some persisted into the nineteenth century. There were no fewer than six papermills on the brook. Paper for Bank of England notes was produced, although this was true of a number of mills throughout the country.

The Walled Town of Chepstow

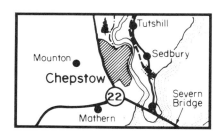

Whether approached from the Gloucestershire side of the Wye, with the view of the great castle spread out on high cliffs, or by passing through the old Town Gate on the Gwent side, Chepstow immediately gives the impression of an ancient town. It derives its name from 'cheap-stowe', a market-place, and it looks like the thriving market town it is, successfully hiding away its industrial area and traces of a once busy port. It was not a large port, but the largest of the small ports that once dotted the Severn up to Gloucester. It had shipbuilding, too, but the increasing size of vessels needed deeper water and greater storage facilities, and these were more adequately provided at the down-channel ports of Avonmouth, Portbury, Newport, Cardiff and Barry.

'The Town Gate' implies that this was a walled town and, indeed, quite a large part of its old walls remain. There is a good view of the wall as you descend into Chepstow from the Severn Bridge and quite an extensive continuation forming the boundary of the town car-park. The walls did not encircle the town but formed a semi-circle, with the river guarding the unwalled boundary, dominated by the castle. However, there is no pedestrian walkway round the top of the walls as in York and Chester.

The oldest building in Chepstow is the castle, built soon after the Norman Conquest, probably not so much as a vital defence but as a base from which Norman troops could push on into Wales, and from this base the Norman lord, William fitz Osbern quickly subdued the larger part of Gwent. The original part of the castle, known as Striguil, was built by fitz Osbern on the narrowest part of the ridge, between the Wye and the present town in

Chepstow Castle

the central part of the present castle site. The Great Tower was the major part of his castle and still stands today, though roofless and floorless. Originally it was of two floors with the hall on the first floor and storage cellar on ground level. The holes for the first-floor rafters are clearly seen. Here lived the lord, his family and retainers. There was a bailey or courtyard on either side.

At the end of the twelfth century, the castle was approached by a gateway in a wall crossing the ridge at the eastern end of the lower of the two courtyards. During the thirteenth century an additional bailey was added at the eastern end, and more commodious and comfortable accommodation was built within its walls. The entrance was now further east. The quarters in the Great Tower were extended by the addition of an upper floor above the original hall, and this hall itself was brightened by putting in larger windows. A further enclosure, known as the barbican, was made at the western end of the site. The thirteenth century also saw the construction of the massive Great Gatehouse, the present public entrance, with its two flanking towers with quarters for guards and prisoners. The Great Tower still

dominates the rest of the castle buildings, and its solid, thick walls have withstood the passage of time better than the thirteenth-century residence.

William fitz Osbern, Earl of Hereford, who started the building in 1067, was succeeded by his son, Roger de Breteuil. Roger was involved in rebellion and lost both his earldom and the castle, and it remained a royal possession until about 1115, when Henry I granted it to Walter fitz Richard de Clare. It remained with the Clare family until 1306, when Roger Bigod III died. He had been in financial difficulties and had obtained a life annuity from Edward I against the surrender of the castle on his death, and so in 1306 it was again in royal hands. In 1312 it was granted to Edward II's half-brother Thomas of Brotherton, and in 1323 Hugh de Despenser the younger, a favourite of Edward II, leased it, with other castles, probably with a view to strengthening his hand against his enemies, but three years later he was captured with the King at Llantrissant and hanged at Hereford.

In 1399 Thomas Mowbray, Marshal of England, came into possession of Chepstow Castle but, supported by Scrope,

Archbishop of York, he raised rebellion against Henry IV, a rebellion which failed and sent both of them to the scaffold. The castle was granted to Mowbray's brother, John, in 1413, and in 1468 his grandson exchanged it with the Earl of Pembroke for other possessions. The Earl's granddaughter, the heiress, married the Earl of Worcester, and the castle remained one of the properties of the same family, earls of Worcester and dukes of Beaufort, until 1914, when it was bought by W. R. Lysaght; in 1955 D. R. Lysaght, his son, conveyed it to the Ministry of Works.

The castle was garrisoned from time to time and, in 1644, when it was held on behalf of King Charles I, it was under threat of siege by the Parliamentarians. They transferred 1,300 troops from Monmouth for the purpose and were about to start the siege when they received news that Monmouth was being attacked by Royalists, who presumably had taken advantage of the depletion of the garrison there. The respite was not for long: in 1645 the castle fell to a Parliamentarian attack. In 1648 it was again a Royalist stronghold, and it came under heavy gunfire from Cromwell's troops. The curtain wall was breached and the castle taken. After the Civil War, it was not 'slighted' like most of the castles in England, including Bristol's, and was garrisoned during the Commonwealth and the Restoration – in fact, until 1690, when it was dismantled. At the restoration Charles II gave the castle back into the control of the Pembroke family.

The castle has had its share of prisoners. Edward II was there for six days before his transfer to his final prison at Berkeley Castle. Perhaps the best-known prisoners were there at the time of the Commonwealth and the Restoration. Bishop Jeremy Taylor, a favourite of Archbishop Laud, a friend of Evelyn the diarist and at one time chaplain to Charles I, was imprisoned in the castle from May to October 1655, but it is not clear on what charge, although presumably for his anti-Puritan views. He had already served one sentence for that reason, and from 1657 to 1658 he was in the Tower of London, apparently through no fault of his own but for his publisher's addition to his *Collection of Offices* of a print showing Christ at prayer.

Perhaps the most interesting of the prisoners was Henry Marten, a Member of Parliament during Charles I's reign, expelled from the House in 1643 for his extreme anti-Royalist speeches but allowed back in 1646. As a signatory to the death warrant of Charles I, he was imprisoned in Chepstow Castle at the Restoration and spent twenty years there, until his death in

1680. Like most regicides, he was sentenced to death, but on his appeal the sentence was commuted to life imprisonment.

Marten lived in quite comfortable quarters in the tower in the south-east corner of the castle site, close to the Great Gatehouse, the tower known today as Marten's Tower. It was entered from the lower bailey, where it was safeguarded by a portcullis, and consisted of a cellar and three storeys, with several rooms and a small chapel. Fireplaces show that there was some degree of comfort, as do the large windows, inserted in places to replace the original arrow slits. Although it is floorless, we can see the interior from several stages, and a walk round the roof parapet gives good views of the castle and town. On each merlon or raised part of the embattlement stands a stone figure, and from below these give an impression of sentries.

In this tower, Henry Marten lived under a kind of house arrest. His movements were restricted, but he lived in the tower with his family and was allowed not only to receive friends but to dine out with them in their own homes in the neighbourhood. He was free to carry on his writing and in 1662 wrote *Henry Marten's Familiar Letters to his Lady of Delight*, a work which incorporated letters he had written to one Mary Ward, his mistress – letters which implied that the ardent Puritan was not the strict moralist he seemed.

Marten was buried nearby in the fine Norman church of St Mary. Originally he was buried in the chancel, but in the eighteenth century a vicar, Thomas Chest, objected to the regicide's being buried in such a sacred part of the church, and the body was removed to its present position in the entrance vestibule under a carpet adjoining the alcove which houses the font. In fact, it could not be any further from the altar. Marten's epitaph reads:

> **H**ere or elsewhere (all's one to you to me)
> **E**arth, air or water grips my ghostless duty
> **N**one knows how soon to be by fire set free
> **R**eader, if you an oft tried rule will trust
> **Y**ou'll gladly do and suffer what you must
> **M**y time was spent in serving yours and you
> **A**nd death's my pay (it seems), and welcome too
> **R**evenge destroying but itself, while I
> **T**o birds of prey leave my old cage and fly.
> **E**xamples preach to the eye. Care then (mine says)
> **N**ot how you end, but how you spend your days
> Aged 78 years.

By reading down the initial letter of each line, it will be seen that they form the name 'Henry Marten'. The lines are said to have been written by him.

The church of St Mary was a priory church, part of a monastic settlement. It was the policy of the Normans to set up monasteries under the protection of a castle. These establishments were often occupied by monks who had come over from Normandy in the wake of the Norman army. They were, however, not independent of their mother house in Normandy, which laid down the discipline to be followed by the daughter house. The new establishments were endowed by their lord and others with land, farms and mills but part of their rents went back to Normandy for the maintenance of the mother house. In course of time many of the monasteries established in England became very rich, until their income ceased in the sixteenth century by Henry VIII's Dissolution of the Monasteries. Generally the monastic buildings were sold off and either pulled down for building-materials or made into secular buildings, except the church or part of it which served the local community, and so St Mary's at Chepstow became the parish church.

William fitz Osbern, the builder of Chepstow Castle, had also built and endowed a Benedictine abbey at Cormeilles in Normandy, the mother house of the priory at Chepstow. It is interesting to note that a 'twinning' relationship has grown up in recent years between the peoples of Cormeilles and Chepstow, and a stone from the now ruinous abbey in Normandy has been presented to Chepstow and now stands in St Mary's Church.

The splendid western front of St Mary's Church, with its fine door and the three windows above, constitutes a delightful Norman façade. The windows have the typical half-round tops with the door frame enclosing the semi-circular tympanum and a cluster of colonnettes on each side. Norman or Romanesque is the type of architecture I admire most for its strength and simplicity and so I am particularly fond of St Mary's. Originally there was a central tower but, like many ancient church towers, it collapsed. That was in 1700, and so in 1705–6 the present tower over the west front was built, but as the magnificent west doorway and windows above catch the eye, the later tower does not detract from the overall impression.

The large car-park just above the church gives a fine view of both the side of the church and the castle, the two principal buildings in Norman times. Once, from here, the port wall, built to protect the castle, the priory and the growing settlement, would have been visible above the small dwellings, but it is now concealed by the later higher buildings. Fortunately the west front is still seen to advantage from the space in front of the church.

Inside the church are the remains of the original impressive Norman nave. Although the end of the nave had to be rebuilt, due in part to the collapse of the tower, no attempt was made to reproduce the Norman work, which might have been confusing to visitor and expert alike. Quite extensive renovations have been made to the church due to natural decay and the presence of the deathwatch beetle, but the work has been carried out in a most enlightened way.

There is much of interest inside the church. The simple grave slab or ledger stone in the floor marking Henry Marten's burial-place is a contrast to the elaborate sixteenth-century 'Worcester tomb', just inside the nave on the left, where Henry, the second Earl of Worcester and his wife, Elizabeth, are buried. The two effigies, in their coronation robes, have been freshly picked out in colours, as they would have been when the tomb was erected. Another large monument with its colours restored is the seven-teenth-century tomb in the south transept to Thomas Shipman and his wife Margaret, who after his death in 1620 married Richard Cleyton, also shown here, along with Margaret's twelve children.

A more recent event is the subject of a painting of the ill-fated attack on Gallipoli in the First World War. The Victoria Cross was awarded posthumously to Seaman Williams of Chepstow, who was killed in the engagement and whose story is well documented in the Chepstow Museum. The painting hangs on the west wall of the Lady Chapel, which has been designated as a war memorial. On the floor at the south side of the nave is the mechanism of the eighteenth-century clock, replaced in the tower in 1966 by an electric clock.

Except by river, the Town Gate, was once the only way into the town, and it makes an impressive entry. It was rebuilt in 1524 and was presented to the town in 1911 by the Duke of Beaufort. At one time it was used as a small prison or lock-up. There was once heavy traffic congestion at the Town Gate, but the present one-way system has now overcome this problem, although traffic queues still occur at times at the river bridge, where traffic can

The Town Gate, Chepstow

proceed in only one direction at a time because of the narrowness
of the bridge.

The Gate House, adjoining the Town Gate, was built in 1609
for Margaret Cleyton but, as it was refaced in the eighteenth
century, it has lost its original appearance. It was common
enough in the eighteenth century to modernize timber-framed
houses by treating them in this way, and many a fine timbered
building hides its face behind a mask of brick or stucco.

Chepstow has two ancient almshouses, the Powys Almshouses,
1716, on the corner at the top of Bridge Street, named after the
founder, Thomas Powys, and the Montague Almshouses in
nearby Upper Church Street. This gabled building was provided
by the generosity of Sir Walter Montague in 1614.

In the nineteenth century Chepstow possessed over seventy
public houses, sometimes so close together that they formed
terraces. All had different names, so if you thought of a pub name,
Chepstow mostly likely had it, and the busy pub trade reflected

the busy waterfront. The town has now about fourteen inns, some of them quite old such as the White Lion, the Three Tuns, the Green Dragon and the Beaufort Arms.

The main streets run steeply down towards the river, crossed by a bridge built by John Rastrick in 1816 to replace a wooden one. Down river from this bridge can be seen the railway bridge built by Brunel in 1852. Because of the strains and stresses which bridges have to endure, continuous maintenance is necessary. The 'live load' – that is, the weight of traffic – has increased over the years, and coupled with 'impact', the strain due to increasing speed, causing extra vibration, has caused maintenance problems. In 1962 the Great Western Railway authorities had to strengthen and alter the bridge so that what you see today is not all Brunel's work. Looking at both bridges from a midway point on the river bank, the delicate ironwork of Rastrick's bridge is more pleasing to the eye than the tubular supports of the railway bridge.

It was by the riverside, of course, that Chepstow's industrial development began, when transport was mainly by water. It was here, too, that the Wye Tour ended. The quiet river frontage, complete with a small public garden, was once thriving with sea-borne traffic, when boats had less draft than today. Warehouses, which once held goods passing through the port, are now abandoned or used for other purposes. There was once even a customs house on the quayside. Bordeaux wines are no longer shipped into Chepstow as they were in the thirteenth century, when the lords of Striguil were allowed to collect the dues, and Bristol now remains the wine port for Bordeaux. A great many other goods once passed through Chepstow. It was a port for industries that then thrived in the Wye Valley, such as the wire- and paperworks round the Tintern area. Wood and coal were shipped down from the Forest of Dean, and stone was also exported. Along the river front were the activities associated with shipping, chandlers, boat-repairers and even shipbuilding, and there was a dry dock, now filled in.

A revival of its shipbuilding activities came in the 1914–18 war, when Chepstow became a National Shipyard. New ships were urgently required to replace those lost by enemy action, and the shipyard was augmented by a new one on the site of the present Army Apprentices' College on the Beachley peninsula. Chepstow was known as Shipyard No. 1, and Beachley as Shipyard No. 2. In 1920 both shipyards were sold. The Chepstow Yard passed to the

Fairfield Engineering & Shipbuilding Company Ltd, later to become Fairfield Mabley Ltd, bridge-builders and structural engineers, whose contribution in the 1960s was the construction of the steel box components which form the M4 roadway of the Severn Bridge. They were made in Chepstow and floated down the Wye to be hoisted into position.

In the shipping days the area round the Boat Inn was known as 'the Devil's Half Acre' because of its bad reputation as a haunt of prostitution, but now, with its riverside walk and seats, it has a definite air of respectability. One of the riverside properties has been converted into the Willow Tree Restaurant, named from the willow tree growing on the adjoining river bank.

On the wall of the building is a plaque, which reads: 'From this riverside on 3rd February 1840 John Frost, William Jones and Zephaniah Williams, the convicted leaders of the Chartist March on Newport sailed to begin their transportation to Van Diemens Land (Tasmania)'. These men were involved in a militant section of the Chartist movement which grew up in the nineteenth century to alleviate the harsh conditions of the Industrial Revolution. On 4 November 1839 the militants planned a march on Newport by 5,000 Monmouthshire miners. Another plan was to release from Monmouth Castle Henry Vincent, a Chartist orator, held there for sedition. Their plans failed. The authorities in Newport were warned and in the Westgate Hotel stationed soldiers, who fired on the marchers, and there were many casualties. The leaders were captured and sentenced to death, but the sentence was commuted to transportation. John Frost, who had been Mayor of Newport, after spending fifteen years in Tasmania, lived for some years in Bristol, occasionally lecturing on the horrors of transportation. The plaque was erected by the Chepstow Society and unveiled in 1985 by Alexander Cordell, a novelist who has written about the Chartist movement and the life of the period.

Like many riverside areas, the waterfront has been subject to flooding during exceptionally high tides, and a few protective sandbags can still be seen outside some buildings. The Boat Inn was being renovated and converted into a dwelling in 1985 in accordance with the general uplift of the riverside properties. At the road bridge end there was a neat row of fishing boats on the bank, a reminder that the Wye is a salmon river, but boats were remaining on the bank, because of a curtailment of salmon fishing, due to the reduction in the number of fish in the Wye.

The Bridge, Chepstow

Visitors to the waterfront often remark on the large square hole which can be seen in the cliff face on the Gloucestershire side of the river. 'Gloucester Hole' is a natural cave, but the entrance was enlarged at some time, apparently to enable the interior to be used for storage. The access is only by boat on a convenient tide.

Not far from the waterfront, a short distance up Bridge Street, is the fine Gwy House, built in 1796, now the home of the Chepstow Museum. George Watkins, a surgeon, lived there in the nineteenth century, and in 1907 it became a girls' school. Like many large houses, during the First World War it became a convalescent home for wounded soldiers, and in 1921 the Chepstow and District Hospital. From those days there are exhibits of a hospital bed, hospital equipment and a large plan of the hospital lay-out. Naturally details of the Wye appear among the many photographs and paintings exhibited, including the history of the trow traffic and the Wye Tour. A few bottles and other items refer to Chepstow's former role as a wine port, and model ships and drawings to its once important industry of shipbuilding. Fishing history has a prominent place, particularly the different methods of salmon fishing.

In the museum is a print of an old map of Chepstow, dated 1686, from which we can see that the general layout of the streets was much the same as today's. Then most of the buildings fronted

onto what is now High Street, running downhill from Town Gate to the present Beaufort Square, from where several streets slope down to the river. Some of these, like the cobbled Hocker Hill Street, still retain their medieval character.

Almost adjoining the museum is a recent addition to Chepstow's industries, the glass-cutting, engraving and gilding works of Stuart & Sons, makers of 'Stuart Crystal'. Their premises, in Bridge Street opposite the castle, are fast becoming a tourist attraction, for you can watch the lead crystal being hand-cut, engraved and gilded with nineteen-carat gold, and there is a shop where you can buy the finished article. You may see an engraver adding a coat of arms to a set of drinking glasses, and for a modest fee you can have your own monogram added to certain types. In another part of the workshop, a gilder may be adding a gold edge to another set, awaiting export to an Arab state. Apart from a small amount at Stourbridge, Chepstow is the only workshop of the firm where gilding is done. The staff include local young people trained there in the various processes.

Frederick Stuart was an orphan who learned glassmaking during the 1820s, as a boy at the Redhouse Glassworks, Wordsley, now a glassmaking museum. In 1851 he went into partnership with Richard Mills and Thomas Webb in a new glassworks, the Albert works, adjoining the Redhouse works. The business flourished, specializing in tableware. In 1876 they received a large order to supply Brunel's *Great Eastern* steamship with glassware, and for many years they were suppliers to the shipping business until the RMS *Queen Elizabeth*'s last voyage in 1970. Frederick Stuart had his eye on the Redhouse Glassworks, where he started as a boy. He took over the lease and in 1885 established the firm of Stuart & Sons there, and from then the business has been run by generations of Stuarts. The company set up an additional factory at Aberbargoed in South Wales in 1966, and in 1983 established the studio workshop in Chepstow in the old board school.

The castle, the waterfront, the museum and the glassworks form a corner of Chepstow packed full of interest, with its relics of bygone days and a glimpse of a present-day craft.

The Bridge, Chepstow

4

From Piercefield to Tintern

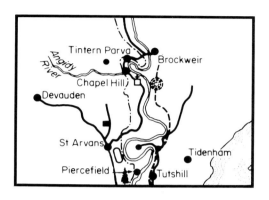

A mile from the centre of Chepstow, a secondary road links up with the main valley road. Adjoining this junction is Lions Gate or Lions Lodge, a striking gateway with lodges on either side and two stone lions crouching on top of high pillars. This was the entrance to the great private estate of Piercefield Park, which once extended as far as Tintern and Devauden. Lions Gate now leads to the stables of the Chepstow Racecourse, opened in 1926 by the Chepstow Racecourse Company, who bought part of Piercefield Park. The public footpath through the wooded area of Piercefield Park nearer the river is by way of the Wye Valley walk from Chepstow which runs near the old mansion and its stables, now in an advanced state of decay. From time to time there have been schemes to make the house into an hotel for the racecourse, but they have come to nothing.

The gateway, its adjoining lodges and the tall wall, now forming the boundary of the racecourse, were built by Sir Mark Wood, owner of Piercefield during the closing years of the eighteenth century. He also completed Piercefield House, which had been largely rebuilt by the previous owner, George Smith, who had been forced to sell due to bankruptcy. Wood added a semi-circular portico to the centre of the three-storeyed house, and with its flanking pavilions at each end it must have been very impressive. Much of the façade still stands, but its interior is now a mere shell. It made a fine show from across the river, as early

Tintern Abbey

prints indicate. A visit to Piercefield was one of the highlights of
the Wye Tour. In fact, a carriage track was made down through
the woods to the river, its course still visible although now
impassable to vehicles.

A great attraction of the grounds in the mid eighteenth century
was that they had been landscaped by Valentine Morris, then the
owner, after the fashion of the day for romantic scenery, as at
Stourhead, Blaise Castle grounds at Bristol and many other
estates. Paths were laid out, viewpoints made with grottoes and
follies; trees were cut down or planted to improve the aspects. It
was an age of landscaped antiquity, of 'druid temples' and
'mysterious standing stones'. Piercefield had its druid temple, a
standing stone or two, a stone giant with his cave and 'awesome
crags'. Their mystery has passed with the times, and so have one
or two of the adornments, but most of the features are still there,
and for the imaginative the present covering of moss and foliage
gives an even more romantic appearance.

There is no general public access to Piercefield Park, but from
time to time you can join one of the walks arranged by the Wye
Valley Warden Service. Also, the public footpath, the Wye Valley
Walk, utilizes part of the Piercefield 'cliff walk', which includes a
number of the features.

When I visited the grounds last, it was with one of the Wye
Valley wardens, and our first stop was at the remains of the ice
house, now only a pit in the ground, partly filled with rubble and
tree debris from the surrounding woodland. Before the days of
refrigeration, the inverted conical pit was filled with ice dragged
up from the frozen river. As the ice melted, it drained out through
straw placed across the small outlet at the base, and the meltwater
was carried away by a subterranean drain, but the supply of ice
lasted through the summer months almost until the first frosts,
and the guest at Piercefield had cool drinks and cold sweets in the
hot weather.

From the ice house we continued by woodland paths down to
the river's edge, pausing on the way to embrace a 'standing stone',
conveniently placed on a footpath. We were told that some people
feel sensations on contact with ancient stones.

At the base of a gulley carrying a stream down towards the
river, we met a small party of mud-covered cave-explorers
who had just emerged from Otter Hole, a fine stalagmite cave
discovered only in recent years, and who told us that the cave
extends under the ice house and for some distance towards the

Old barn, Piercefield

racecourse. The cave is not open to the public and is gated, for it is dangerous to inexperienced explorers, as it is invaded by the Wye at high tide, when parts of the cave are quickly flooded when the incoming tide meets the outgoing stream. Cavers exploring the more distant parts of the cave are unable to get out again until the tide recedes. The cave contains some of the finest and largest formations ever discovered, but it is a muddy cave, because of the tidal water washing in the river mud.

Various holes seen in the wood are not the work of cavers but of manuscript-hunters. The search started about 1909, when Dr Orville Owen of Detroit, a writer and a great advocate of the Bacon-wrote-Shakespeare theory, suggested that the original manuscripts of Shakespeare's (Bacon's) works had been hidden in six watertight lead boxes somewhere in the Chepstow area. His evidence was based on certain clues deduced from the disputed works.

Owen first investigated a cave in the river cliff near Chepstow and, deciding that the manuscripts could well be in the river itself, built a coffer dam. However, though he excavated a lot of mud, nothing was found. In 1920 he turned his attention to Chepstow Castle and carried out an excavation there without success. Back

The Mansion ruins, Piercefield

on dry land, he dug holes in Piercefield's woodland close to the river bank. Since then other people have tried their luck in the same area, but to no avail.

As we walked along the river bank we saw the small church of St James on the Lancaut peninsula opposite, a peninsula formed by a great loop of the Wye. Beyond, the limestone face of Wintour's Leap gleamed in the sun.

During another visit, we went through a tunnel made in the rock which once had a stone figure of a giant over one end of the tunnel, but this had fallen away and disappeared long ago. We were told that it was once customary to knock three times to seek the giant's permission to go through, but since the giant is no longer at home, the procedure is no longer necessary.

What of Valentine Morris who laid out these landscaped pleasure grounds in the mid eighteenth century? The house at Piercefield was purchased by his father, Colonel Valentine Morris, in 1740, and his son inherited it at the age of fifteen, along with vast estates in Antigua, where he was born. He was a very wealthy man, his income coming chiefly from his sugar plantations in Antigua, where he owned a large number of slaves. He was generous to the extreme, but he also liked to frequent the gambling establishments in Bath. He died in London in 1789.

Adjoining Piercefield is the longest straight stretch on the Wye, Longhope Reach, a whole mile without bends, before it makes its final twist.

In early spring, I joined another interesting walk on the other side of the river to the Lancaut peninsula. We met near the top of Wintour's Leap, where a sheer drop gives a fine view of the double loop of the Wye below, and descended a steep woodland path to the bank of the river, passing two contiguous limekilns. (There are many in the valley, as farmers used to prepare their own lime.) The path descended through wild daffodils and primroses, and on the river bank were beds of wild violets and clusters of buddleia trees, promising swarms of summer butterflies. On the edge of the river, wooden piles were sticking out of the mud, showing where the boats used to tie up for the river trade.

The riverside settlements at Lancaut have now disappeared, and their sites are distinguishable only by aerial photographs. Local tradition says that they were abandoned because of an outbreak of plague, but they may have become deserted when the river trade ran down. Their church is still there, the little church of St James, now roofless and ruinous but still beautiful in its lovely setting near the Wye. The Lancaut Church Preservation Group aims to make the walls safe and to carry out a thorough archaeological survey before repairing the structure, and no doubt much vital information about its history will result from this work. It was originally the Celtic church of St Cewydd, founded about AD 700, and one part still shows Saxon features. The Normans extended it in the early twelfth century and re-dedicated it to St James, then a fashionable dedication because of the cult of St James of Compostela. It is said that during the Middle Ages it probably served the religious needs of lepers from a nearby hospital. Its greatest treasure is a late twelfth-century lead font, one of six in Gloucestershire, all of the same design and made from the same mould. There are only thirty lead fonts of that period in the whole of England and Wales. That from Lancaut is now safely housed in the Lady Chapel of Gloucester Cathedral. An old tombstone rests against one of the church's interior walls: 'Here Lyeth the Body of Jane the wife of Henry Stephens' and underneath a memorial to Henry Stephens; the dates are obliterated but are possibly both 1683.

Back on the Gwent side of the river, high above the road to Tintern, is Wyndcliff, one of the attractions of the Wye Tour. The top of the great cliff can be reached by the very long flight of stone steps from the road or by taking a minor marked road from St Arvans to a woodland car-park and then following the upward winding footpath to the ridge. Here, 700 feet above the river, are

Wyndcliff, the 365 steps

magnificent views, and it is said that on a fine day you can see parts of Gwent, Glamorgan, the Brecon Beacons in Powis, Gloucestershire, Avon, Wiltshire, Somerset, Hereford & Worcester, including the Malvern Hills, and even Devon, if you are lucky.

The footpath leads to the top of the steps. They were first constructed in 1828–9 under the instructions of the Duke of Beaufort, the landowner. They are known as the 365 Steps, although the number has been reduced by repairs and renewals. (Those who count them usually end up with conflicting numbers.) Near the top is a rock platform with a parapet and seat, erected to the memory of Chris Pugh, a Wye Valley warden well known for his devotion to the area. This viewpoint is known as 'the Eagle's Nest' and was a highlight of the Wye Tour for the view of the many counties. Whether you go up the steps or down them is a matter of personal choice, and those who are not keen on heights would probably prefer the ascent. They do not go up vertically but by a series of gradients and are quite safe with a reasonable amount of care on the irregular edges; like all steps they can be slippery in bad weather. A great deal of work in the Wye Valley has been initiated by the Lower Wye Valley Preservation Society, to whom we owe a debt for safeguarding many of the features of the lower Wye – the preservation of these steps is an example. They in conjunction with the Nature Conservancy, the Forestry Commission and the Monmouthshire Countryside Committee, have restored the steps in recent years, with the Army Apprentices' College at Beachley providing the labour.

At the bottom of the steps was once Moss Cottage, now demolished, with a roof of thatched heather and walls covered with moss. Its rustic appearance was enhanced by a verandah with rough tree-trunk columns; beneath the verandah, or on the open space in front, visitors could picnic or fortify themselves for the ascent or recover from the descent by taking refreshments. A small charge was made at the cottage for the use of the steps. In 1909 it was 6d, but there is no charge today.

To the north the Tintern road follows close to the river. On both sides vertical faces of bare rock show up among the trees. It is a winding road, and suddenly, round a bend, the impressive ruins of Tintern Abbey appear on the watermeadow adjoining the road.

Ruined cottage seen from Tintern Abbey

It stands roofless and windowless, a beautiful ruined abbey. The site was cleaned up on the Duke of Beaufort's orders before 1901, and the succeeding owners, the Ministry of Works, now the Department of the Environment, have done their share of restoration, stone-cleaning and removing the ivy. Dank woods, moss-covered stones and ivy-clad ruins were all ingredients of the Wye Tour in the eighteenth and early nineteenth centuries. At the time of the Tour, writers wrote of the poor hovels built up against the interior walls of the abbey church, and the beggars, who pestered them for money as guides, were curiosities in themselves. The boat passengers would partake of a robust meal at the Beaufort Hotel, originally called the Beaufort Arms, or spread their tablecloths on the floor of the abbey church and eat their poultry and salmon and display their bottles of wine oblivious to the poor people around them. Today there are many more visitors thronging the abbey, but the hovels and beggars have gone, and the coach horses, waiting in the Beaufort Hotel stables to take back visitors to Monmouth, have been replaced by the cars packing the car-parks to the side of the abbey.

It was not unknown for visitors to view the ruins by torchlight, a kind of *son et lumière* without the *son*, and it was considered romantic to do so by moonlight. In fact, after the railway was built, special excursions were arranged for this purpose. More recently, it is said, a party of Japanese visitors were told by their guide that, at that time of the year, the full moon shone through one of the round windows of the abbey, producing quite a spectacular effect. They persuaded the guide to take them for a night visit and, as the moon rose, expressed their delight – in, of course, Japanese. The next morning the news spread that ghostly chanting in an unknown tongue had been heard coming from the abbey church. Could it be the ancient monks assembled for a ghostly Mass, chanting in Latin?

The abbey was founded in 1131 for the Cistercians, a Benedictine splinter group following the stricter rule of the earlier Benedictines in accordance with practices at the abbey at Cîteaux in France. The first Cistercian house in England had been established in Surrey only three years before. Although the abbey's foundation was 1131, the present ruins are of the larger, thirteenth-century building which replaced it. The new abbey was built to the south of the original abbey to enable services to continue during rebuilding. Edward II stayed at the abbey for two nights in 1326, when in flight from his vengeful Queen and her lover, Roger Mortimer.

Like other abbeys, it finally fell victim to Henry VIII's Dissolution of the Monasteries. The lead and bells were sold; the buildings gradually fell into ruins and have remained so ever since. The most imposing part of the monastic ruins is the Abbey Church, as most of its main walling, including the four great pointed gables, one at each end of the cruciform building and one at the end of each transept, still stand to roof level. The Cistercians were an austere order and their churches were free from elaborate carving and decoration, but in spite of its simplicity, the immensity of the Abbey Church at Tintern is certainly impressive. The enormous opening of the east window, with views of the countryside, is an outstanding feature. Much of the internal tracery which once held the glass has gone, but this is little loss, as in a Cistercian church, decorative glass would have been kept to a minimum.

North of the church can be seen the foundations of many other monastic buildings, the great cloister and the rectangular chapter house where the abbey business was transacted. North of the great cloister were the domestic buildings, used as sleeping quarters, dining rooms and kitchens, with the small warming room, where a fire was kept at all hours, the only source of warmth for the monks. To the east was the infirmary, where the sick and aged were cared for, with their own cloister and kitchen.

The ruins vary in date from the twelfth to the fifteenth centuries, so several types of stone have been used in construction, mostly Devonian sandstone quarried locally on the edge of the Forest of Dean. Other finer local stones were used for mouldings and other carvings, including Dundry stone, an oolite from the Bristol area. Purple sandstone and pink quartz conglomerate can be found on the site. After the Dissolution, the abbey and a vast surrounding area were granted to the Earl of Worcester; in 1682 the Marquis of Worcester, who owned Monmouth Castle and built the great Castle House there, was created Duke of Beaufort, and Tintern remained in the Beaufort family until in 1901 the abbey and the surrounding area were sold to the Crown.

The area covered by the monastery included the site of the seventeenth-century Anchor Hotel, on the east side of the car-parks. Here you can see the abbey gateway leading down to the river bank where the monks had their ferry across the river. There was still a ferry here during part of the present century. The

eastern boundary crossed what is now the Chepstow-Monmouth road, which did not exist until about 1820. The boundary then ran behind the Beaufort Hotel and the adjoining house, St Annes, a modern building incorporating the old monastic gatehouse chapel. The monastic gatehouse stood where the gateway to the drive is today. The boundary still continued down the right-hand side of the lane adjoining the house, meeting the Chepstow-Monmouth road again, and crossed the road to join the western boundary of the site.

Although the abbey ruins are a great tourist attraction, with the inevitable refreshment places and a Welsh Tourist Board information office, the remainder of Tintern is still a fairly quiet village, mainly strung along the Chepstow-Monmouth road which becomes busy during the tourist season. There are a few small shops, one or two with ice-cream and postcards opposite the parking bay by the river, but these are unobtrusive and serve the local population as well as the tourist trade. There is little tourist development, no amusement arcade, but there are several hotels and inns near the abbey site and in the village. No doubt it is the quiet ecclesiastical atmosphere of the abbey and the strict planning control which have preserved the village.

There were once thirteen taverns in Tintern, and there are now eight, although because of the growth of tourism some have developed into hotels. Local residents remember the time when only the Beaufort and the Rose & Crown were hotels and the others mainly cider houses, and speak of Captain Sharpe, a tenant of the Beaufort who had two tame otters – the female, Bella, would follow him to the Wye, where she would swim and sometimes catch fish, but she would always follow him home again. He had a fishpond in which Bella loved to swim, but she would never touch any of his goldfish.

During the last war there were many evacuees in Tintern and the surrounding district. It was considered a safe area, but there was some war damage. One enemy bomb, apparently dumped after a bombing raid elsewhere, demolished a bungalow belonging to a Mr Arnold, known locally as 'the beekeeper'. Fortunately there were no casualties, but it was an alarming experience.

The wire-, iron- and brassworks once at Tintern have gone, with the clatter of their machinery and the industrial traffic on the Wye. The industry lasted here for 3½ centuries and did not die out until 1901. There was even a works adjoining the abbey, and similar works spread up the Angidy river for nearly two miles.

Tintern Abbey

Tintern across the river

Although it was originally intended to produce brass in the area, it was quickly superseded by iron, a cheaper and speedier process with the raw materials available locally. Little evidence can now be seen of industrial sites, although most of the ponds associated with them still remain, as do the ruins of the Angidy ironworks. Many works used water-power, but waterwheels have been broken up long since, except one, associated with a former sawmill, which in 1985 was being preserved and restored, adjoining the main road. I was told that in the 1930s Jack Jones, who owned the Tintern sawmills, used to produce a thousand chair-legs for half a crown.

Water was only used not for industry: at the Moon & Sixpence, an inn on the main road, a stream flowed over the beer barrels and kept them cool. The Moon & Sixpence was once called the Masons' Arms, but the name was changed by a previous owner, an admirer of Somerset Maugham, who wrote a novel of that name.

There are a number of walks round Tintern, including part of the Wye Valley Walk. One short walk with wonderful views is up to the ruined church of St Mary, which can be seen on the side of the hill overlooking Tintern. The way to the church is by the lane opposite the entrance to the abbey car-park. At the bottom of the

Ruins of St Mary's church, Chapel Hill

lane are a Wye Valley Walk sign and a wall postbox. Opposite the
house, St Tewdrik, a cobbled way ascends the hill and is an
example of what an old 'paved' road was like in the days of travel
by horseback and coaches. The way ascends steadily after a sharp
bend until you come to a seat with fine views over Tintern and the
river. It continues through woodland as a marked track, the
Chapel Hill and Barbadoes Walk, but a quickly ascending path,
opposite the seat, brings you into the churchyard and to the tower
of St Mary's Church, with its saddle roof, the only roofed part of
the church, for it was destroyed by fire some ten or more years
ago, with the tragic death of some local men. The church was built
in 1886 on the site of a previous church, as is seen from the dates of
some of the early tombstones, such as those of the Rose family,
from 1720 to 1819, by the side of the path to the church. The
churchyard is very much overgrown, with stones leaning in
various directions, and the ground is much pitted. Through the

swirling mists of winter, it is a scene of ghostly desolation, yet in early spring there are great patches of snowdrops in the entanglement of ground growth. A feature of the walk is the particularly splendid view, from the churchyard wall, of Tintern Abbey in the valley below.

Although St Mary's Church served the people of Chapel Hill and the abbey end of Tintern, the other end of the village, at Tintern Parva, was served by the parish church of St Michael near the river bank, the church which is now used by the whole of the village. It is reached by a narrow road which descends towards the river between some houses – in fact, by two narrow roads which form a triangle, a small compact area, between the Chepstow-Monmouth road and the river. No wonder they call it 'Little Tintern'. There are two interesting benefaction notices on the church wall: one concerns a gift in 1654 of rents to assist 'poor housekeepers' of the parishes of Chapel Hill and Tintern, the other a legacy of £6 a year to enable a poor boy to be apprenticed, from the clerk of the then wireworks, Francis Bradford, who died in 1657.

The old Tintern railway station is at Tintern Parva, a mile above the abbey towards Monmouth. It is between the river and the main road, where there is a prominent direction sign to the information centre and picnic ground. The picnic area is in fact part of the old station, and there are the usual station buildings, with the waiting-room serving refreshments in the summer season, platform, signalbox and platform-ticket machine. However, you could wait for ever for a train, because the line closed for passengers in 1959 and for commercial traffic in 1964. The signalbox is now an information office and a base for the Wye Valley Warden Service, under the joint control of the Gwent and Gloucestershire County Councils. Information about guided and unguided walks and many pamphlets, books and maps of the area are to be found here. Although the signal equipment has been removed from the signalbox, operational levers have been installed near the base of the steps and now are probably more in use than they ever were in the days of the rail traffic, for there are always children around them to operate the levers and see the signal arm move into position. There is a railway carriage with an exhibition of photographs of the history of the Wye industry and railway, and one end of the carriage is a small lecture-room where talks, with slides and films about the valley, are given at certain times.

The old railway station, Tintern

The line, originally the Wye Valley line, later part of the Great Western Railway and laid down in 1876, was a single track, and the island platform formed a loop to await clearance of up and down trains. The train ride up the valley must have been a very scenic one, and it is a pity it has gone, for train passengers see a different aspect of the countryside. Fields, farms and river hardly seen from the road are visible and, free from the steering wheel, the passenger can sit back and enjoy the scenery.

The platform-ticket box at the side of the station is still there for you to pay a nominal fee for parking. Many people use this car-park and picnic ground as a base for walks around Tintern and on the other side of the river, for you can cross over by the bridge at Brockweir and by the old railway bridge at Tintern. An easy walk across the river is the Monks' Path, said to be the path taken by the Tintern monks to visit their grange at Brockweir. The walk runs near the river on slightly higher ground with fine views across the valley. Across the old railway bridge is the steep walk to the Devil's Pulpit, a natural rock formation, high up on the east side of the valley, adjoining Offa's Dyke path, where a footpath joins it from the Tidenham direction. Here the Devil is said to have sat and preached bawdy sermons to the monks of

Tintern to tempt them from their virtuous life, but the monks seem to have been content with their austere rule in this fertile valley, sheltered by the great wooded cliffs to the east and to the west.

Signals at the old railway station, Tintern

Devauden, Trellech and St Briavels

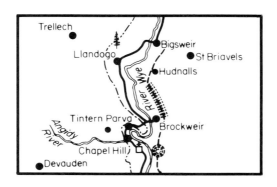

If we climb these wooded heights to the west of Tintern up the Angidy river, further into Wales, taking the left-hand fork to the old road to Monmouth, we eventually reach Devauden, although the more direct route from the south is by St Arvans. It is a somewhat scattered village, described at the beginning of the nineteenth century as a settlement of small farmers, quarrymen, mule-drivers and labourers, who held their cottages from the landowner, the Duke of Beaufort. At that time some of the inhabitants were noted for their dishonesty, as people were in remote places where there was no lord of the manor to keep order. There was no local church, the nearest being at Kilgwrrwg, and Sir Thomas Phillips, who wrote about Devauden at the time, said even that was little used – on only twelve Sundays in the year, after cleaning out the filth left by cattle and sheep which occupied it for the rest of the time. The devout had to go to the parish church at Newchurch.

In 1739 John Wesley chose Devauden Green for his first open-air service, and tradition has it that he was thrown into the village pond. However, his name is preserved today in Wesley Way. Nonconformist movements were becoming well established by the beginning of the nineteenth century, and no fewer than five

chapels were eventually provided in the immediate neighbourhood. Methodism and other Nonconformist bodies were then
considered a serious threat to the Established Church, and this
was one of the reasons for the renovation of older churches and the
building of new churches during the nineteenth century.

Perhaps this was why the village schoolmaster, James Davies,
set up in Devauden a place of worship for the Established Church.
From 1815, when the local schoolroom was built, Davies had
included religion among his subjects, but in 1827 he managed to
get the schoolroom licensed for evening services, and in 1829 the
first full service was held, with a congregation of more than
200 filling the hall which was originally intended for 120 children.
The schoolroom was designated a 'chapel of ease', so baptism
and the provision of a burial-ground remained the prerogative
of the parish church at Newchurch. It was not until 1958 that the
Devauden Chapel became a church in its own right, dedicated to
St James. Marriages could now be solemnized, but the land
attached is very small and no inhumation burials are made at
Devauden, though a small plot is reserved for cremation burials.

The plain glass Gothic-type windows, a porch and other
external features were additions made to the schoolroom to give it
a more church-like appearance, and a vestry was added. The
interior is simple, light and airy, and the only coloured glass is
that of a small war-memorial window behind the altar. In the
early days box pews were introduced, but these have been
removed. A hook in a ceiling beam is pointed out as one from
which a basket was suspended in the old schoolroom days, in
which a naughty child would be placed and hoisted aloft, away
from the other children – a practice not restricted to Devauden.

James Davies devised various fund-raising schemes to fulfil his
ambition for a church at Devauden. One was collecting rags to
sell to papermakers at Mounton, which earned him the name of
'Jemmy the Rag', a nickname which shows that on this far west
side of the valley we are getting into a district of Welsh origins and
culture. There is little Welsh spoken, but English is spoken with a
soft Welsh intonation and turn of phrase, such as the coupling of a
name with occupation. A young Welsh friend told me that she
could not make up her mind whether to marry 'Dai the Milk' or
'Dai the Bread', and I knew of a lady called 'Elsie the Bull', a
strange combination of the sexes, but the truth was that her father
kept 'The Bull' public house.

An old Welsh custom still kept up at Devauden is that of the

The Virtuous Well, Trellech

calennig. An apple is chosen for its red skin, and a sprig of holly is pushed in at the top, from which hang raisins and small fruit. Hazel twigs, covered with silver paper one pushed into the base of the apple, and small pieces of coloured paper decorate the skin. The apple stands for a fruitful life and when rotted is thrown away, but as long as it is kept it is said to bring good luck to the household.

The old part of Devauden is round Devauden Green, and a little further down the road is the Beaufort Aviary, with its rare pheasants, geese, ducks, peacocks and other birds. Like most villages, Devauden has changed since the nineteenth century. Some of the old cottages have gone, others are modernized and there are some new houses and bungalows, with a share of commuters and retired people. The present junior school adjoins the church, and older children travel to Chepstow or Monmouth.

Some five miles to the north of Devauden, on the old road to Monmouth, is Trellech, and although there may have been Seven Wonders of the World, Trellech has three of its own, a standing stone alignment, an enormous mound and a Virtuous Well.

The three prehistoric standing stones known as 'Harold's

Church of St Nicholas from behind the Terret Mound, Trellech

Stones' are almost equally spaced at about twenty paces apart in one line. They are also described as 'the Devil's Arrows' but maybe 'Trellech Stones' is more appropriate, as they have nothing to do with Harold or the Devil. It is not known why they were erected, but they are part of a huge assembly of such monuments scattered all over the British Isles. Archaeologists assign them to the Bronze Age, about 3,500 years ago, long before Harold the Saxon King.

The Trellech Stones belong to the time of the stone circles, solitary standing stones and lines of standing stones, known as henges, menhirs and alignments. Although there are now only three stones at Trellech, there may have been more originally and, unless it has already been done, a proper scientific search in the area for filled-in stone holes might be justified. It has been suggested that alignments and solitary standing stones were direction-finders at a time when people made their way across open country and moorland. The Trellech alignment is not unique to Wales. On the mountain above Dan yr Ogof Caves in the Swansea Valley is the Saith Maen, the Welsh name meaning 'Seven Stones'. Trellech's name is probably derived from the

Welsh words '*tri*' for 'three' and '*llech*' for 'slab'. The name seems to suffer from a variety of spellings even today.

The large mound on Court Farm is no less than 450 feet in diameter and is known as 'the Terret'. It has been described as possibly a burial mound or tumulus, but it is large for an average-size burial mound and is more likely to be a motte, the supporting mound of a Norman castle. There are adjoining traces of other earthworks, which could confirm the layout of a Norman motte and bailey, a type of fortification common in the border area.

The third wonder of Trellech is the Virtuous Well, no doubt an early pagan well once revered as the abode of a local spring deity and later Christianized in the name of a saint, as St Anne at Trellech, for early missionaries tried to stop the heathen worship at these wells, or springs, by designating saints to them. But superstition still surrounds them, and there is the belief that, if you throw a stone into the Virtuous Well and bubbles rise up, your wish will be fulfilled. Another belief is that the water is good for eye complaints.

The well is found adjoining the Tintern to Trellech road. Just before the village there is a nameboard for Trellech and sufficient space to park a car. Opposite is a pedestrian gate with a direction board, and in a hollow of the field there is the Virtuous Well. It was restored to commemorate the Festival of Britain, 1951, and is enclosed by a low circular wall with an entrance gap and a stone bench round the interior. Opposite the entrance is a small niche enclosing the well itself. The floor is of slabs covered with water with a surface of green weed when the feeder spring is full. At other times the paving is dry, with a little water welling up between the slabs.

A sundial is an unusual piece of church furniture, but there is one in the parish church of St Nicholas at Trellech. It is dated 1689 and is inscribed with the three curiosities of Trellech. It once stood outside the church but was brought inside to preserve it from the weather. The church is mainly of the thirteenth and fifteenth centuries, although it is believed to be of Norman origin. The Early English arcading belongs to the thirteenth century, but the clerestory above was added in the fifteenth century, when there was such a spate of rebuilding and 'improvement' to churches that much earlier church architecture was destroyed. In 1792 the church tower partly collapsed, destroying at least part of the nave roof. A lower roof was then constructed, leaving that

familiar tell-tale outline on the external wall of the tower where a higher roof once joined. It was not unusual for church towers to collapse, as often the foundations were not taken down to bed-rock.

The coat of arms displayed in the church is that of Charles II. After the Restoration, it was ordered that the royal coat of arms be displayed in all churches, but many of them have since been replaced by the Hanoverian arms, so it is pleasing to see the earlier example. The pulpit dates to 1640, in the reign of Charles I, but it is only part of the original tall three-stage, or 'three-decker', pulpit. It is thought that one of the decks is now the pulpit used in Penallt old church, once part of Trellech parish, and another part may be included in the screen of St Catwg, Cwmcarvan. There are three fonts in the church, Saxon, Norman and Early English, the latter the only one in use.

There is a preaching cross in the churchyard, much restored but believed to date from the eighth or ninth century. By the cross is a large stone slab resting on two shaped supports, standing on a similar slab at ground level. Several interpretations have been suggested. One is that it was a druids' altar, but there is no evidence that the druids had altars; another that it was a 'resur-rection' stone – a heavy stone placed over a new grave to prevent the corpse being stolen for anatomical purposes; more probably it is a decorative feature of a grave, particularly as it is said to have had incised crosses on the supports which now seem to have weathered away. Close to the structure are a large number of eighteenth-century tombstones, dating from 1751 and on through the century. They are very clearly engraved and ornately deco-rated, such as the one in front of the churchyard cross to James Pugh, who died in 1777, and his wife Eleanor, with two angel faces above the inscription. The adjoining gravestone is that of Alice, Martha and Mary, their children, one aged nine and the others, presumably twins, aged three, with three angel faces at the head.

Among the ancient buildings of Trellech is Court Farm, prob-ably partly Tudor and probably once the old manor house. There are several old buildings, such as the barn with its arrow-slit-type openings, opposite the Crown Inn. Some of the buildings may have earlier structures behind the present façades. The Crown Inn was once the court house, like many inns throughout the country. The ancient-looking doorway leading into the yard looks a little 'pseudo', as engraved over the opening, where one would expect to find a Latin motto, is the simple word 'Gents'.

The sundial, Trellech

The Preaching Cross, Trellech

Trellech was once a busy town and borough. Fire, death, battle and pestilence have all played their part in reducing it to the quiet country village it is today. The first disaster was in 1291, when as a town it had reached its greatest size, and that disaster was due to deer poaching. The Duke of Norfolk accused the Duke of Hereford of allowing inhabitants of Trellech to poach deer in Norfolk's Chepstow deer park. So enraged was Norfolk that he sent his men to Trellech to burn down the town and kill many of the townspeople. The population that was left repaired much of the damage, and the town began to settle down once more. The fourteenth century saw two further afflictions. One was the Black Death which ravaged the country and may have been brought to Trellech by boatmen bringing goods by river and donkey. The other was the damage done by Owain Glyndwr and his men, who laid waste much of the borderland. As you walk though the peaceful village today, it is sad to remember the scenes of horror which once took place here.

Just above Tintern and within walking distance is Brockweir, on the opposite bank of the Wye. There used to be a ferry, but it made its exit in 1904 when the present bridge was built. There is an attractive walk from the old Tintern station to the bridge, avoiding the main Tintern to Monmouth road. As you walk across the bridge and look at the pleasant buildings ahead, it is difficult to imagine that this small place was once only second to Chepstow as a river port on the Wye. Chepstow thrived, for it was not only close to the Severn but on the main routes from England and Wales, so it was not solely dependent on the declining Wye river trade. Brockweir was also a centre on the river for shipbuilding, mostly boats of under a hundred tons, although in 1824 it dealt with some vessels of a little more tonnage. It also fitted out boats made in other boatyards on the Wye, such as the *Duchess of Beaufort* from the Monmouth yard. Wye trows continued to be built at Brockweir until 1925. The remains of one of the last boats to be moored at Brockweir, a twin-screw vessel, were dug out of the mud in 1967, near the bridge where remains of the quay can still be seen. In the garden of the adjoining Quay House there still remains part of the shaft and screw of the vessel.

One of the advantages of the shipbuilding yard at Brockweir was that the river is tidal up to Brockweir Bridge, and an exceptional spring tide will reach the next bridge up the river at Bigsweir. The trows used to come up the river on the tide and were then manhandled over shallows except where towpaths were provided for horses. Larger vessels of up to ninety tons could negotiate the river from Chepstow to Brockweir. Then the cargoes had to be off-loaded onto barges, and these were hauled further up the river by men and horses. According to *The Tale of a Wye Fisherman* by H. A. Gilbert, one of the last of the 'bow-hauliers' told him that one haulier was needed for every ton of cargo, which meant that a heavy coal barge required twenty hauliers. Haulage was necessary mostly for the coal trows on route for Monmouth and Hereford, but this trade decreased when the railway was built between Gloucester and Hereford. Although metal and paper products were also transported up the Wye from the Tintern area, much of the trade was down stream and across the Bristol Channel.

At one time there were no fewer than sixteen public houses in Brockweir. Nelson is reputed to have stayed at the Royal Arms, when inspecting the Forest of Dean for suitable timber for the Navy. There is no Royal Arms there now but a private residence. Among the old buildings is one which some believe may have been used in the fourteenth century as a grange by the monks at

Brockweir Bridge and Moravian church

Tintern Abbey and known as the Malthouse. An original architectural feature is a small cusped and foiled window opening.

The small Moravian church at Brockweir was built in 1831 by Moravians from Bristol. Like the Cistercians who broke away from the Benedictines to follow a stricter discipline, the Protestant Moravians considered that the Established Church was not sufficiently pious, so they formed their own sect which spread as far as Britain and America. Their little church was not dedicated to a saint, for they did not believe in such dedications, as all churches were dedicated to God.

Near the Moravian church is the grave of Flora Klickmann, close to that of her husband, Ebenezer Henderson Smith. She was at one time editor of, *The Girls' Own Paper*, and he one of the founders of *The Boys' Own Paper*. She was a frequent visitor to Brockweir and, after her marriage, had a house there where she spent much of her spare time, away from the editorial desk in London. There, in the 1920s, she wrote a series of articles for her magazine, based on the area around Brockweir, in which she introduced imaginary local characters. They were the 'Flower Patch' stories and had such appeal that she produced in book form such works as *The Flower Patch among the Hills*, *Between the Larch Woods and the Weir*, *The Flower Patch Garden Book* and others. She died in 1957.

On the same side of the Wye as Brockweir is St Briavels, with its castle, now used as a youth hostel. It has recently come into the charge of the English Heritage and is open on certain days of the year. The grass-covered moat forms a small park, voluntarily maintained by the Moat Society of St Briavels. The castle was probably built in 1131 by Milo Fitzwalter, Earl of Hereford, although the existing remains date from about 1250 or a little later. It was the administrative centre for the Forest of Dean, a royal hunting forest, and the Constable of the Castle not only ensured that the forest laws were kept but provided lodging for the royal visitors who came to hunt. King John was quite a frequent visitor. Today only a fragment of the original buildings remains, mainly the gatehouse with its two flanking D-shaped towers. The central part of the castle, the keep, was in such a ruinous state that it collapsed in the middle of the eighteenth century. Offenders against the forest laws were imprisoned in St Briavels, and between 1670 and 1720 the gatehouse was used as a debtors' prison. Now the Free Miners' Association of the Forest of Dean sometimes meets at the castle, as an alternative to Speech House, where their quarterly meetings are held.

On a couple of occasions, I have had the pleasure of being shown round the castle by Mr L. P. O'Leary, who is in charge of the Youth Hostel. His description and tour of the buildings were both informative and entertaining. He told me in 1984 that he had been a warden there for sixteen years, so he knew the area well. I was shown the room in which King John is reputed to have slept on his visits to the forest, the prison cell, the adjoining guardroom and the dungeon, its windows barred and even the chimney flue barred partway up. Mr O'Leary said that once a young visitor asked how Father Christmas managed! On the plaster of a window recess in the guardroom is scratched '18th May P F 1790' just one of several old graffiti. On one wall of the prison is a drawing of a trow, on another a map which is not easy to see and around which a story has grown up that it marks the position of buried coins. Another intriguing inscription is on the prison wall: 'Robin Belcher the day will come that thou shalt answer for it for thou hast sworn against me 1671.'

The warden, Mr O'Leary, often holds a medieval 'mock court' for the amusement of visitors. Volunteers from the visiting party act as president of the court, the accused, defending counsel and members of the jury, while he takes the part of the prosecutor. The 'accused' is usually found guilty and sentenced to be hanged from the gatehouse or sent to the dungeon, which is entered by a trapdoor, a formidable pit – in French an *oubliette*, from the verb *oublier*, to forget – where the unfortunate culprit could indeed be forgotten.

During the Middle Ages, 'quarrels', bolts used for shooting from crossbows, were made at the castle from Dean iron, and both Henry III and his father, King John, were supplied with thousands of crossbow bolts from this source, while Edward III had 500 iron clubs to help settle troubles in Ireland.

The red sandstone of which the castle is built gives quite a feeling of warmth to the grim building, particularly on a sunny day. This is not a hard stone, like the other stone of the area, the Carboniferous limestone, and the sharp edges soon weather to a pleasing softness.

Opposite, the church is St Mary's, much of it Norman, including the fine Transitional Norman supporting arches which once carried the tower over the crossing, and the font is Norman. Some rebuilding was done in the nineteenth century. A new tower was

St Briavels Castle

built about 1830, and the Early English chancel was rebuilt in 1861. Associated with the church is the unique bread-and-cheese ceremony, which is held after evensong every Whit Sunday. The earliest record of the ceremony is in 1779, when Rudder stated in his *History of Gloucestershire* that every householder in the parish paid a penny towards the expenses, but the tradition is that it was Milo Fitzwalter, Earl of Hereford, who built the original castle at St Briavels, or his wife, who introduced the ceremony, granting to the parishioners the right to cut wood from Hudnalls, a wood between the village and the Wye. This concession was won from him by his wife, who rode round the wood on horseback. Another version says that she imitated Lady Godiva and that King John was so taken with the ceremony that he ordered all the ladies of St Briavels to follow her example. Be that as it may, the parishioners were supposed to have given bread and cheese to the poor in gratitude for the privilege of wood-cutting, although it has been suggested that the bread and cheese were originally issued to the foresters who came fasting to Mass from long distances.

An account in Farley's *Bristol Journal* in 1807 says that pieces of bread and cheese, about one inch square, were thrown from the church gallery, which no longer exists. However, this led to such unruly behaviour in the church that about 1857 it was scattered from the church tower and subsequently in the village outside the church grounds. By the late nineteenth century the pieces of cheese seem to have been reduced to the size of a dice. No doubt the price had increased by then. The right to cut wood from Hudnalls was quoted in 1282 and reiterated in the Dean Forest Reafforestation Act of 1688.

I went along to see for myself the bread-and-cheese ceremony on Whit Sunday 1985. About 7.15 p.m. cars began to park near the church. A 'forester' waiting, like myself, by the church told me that he had been born in the Hundred of St Briavels and had come back, after thirty years away from the Forest, to see the ceremony he remembered from his boyhood days. He told me that people used to keep the pieces they caught and would sleep with them under their pillows to dream of the future, good or bad. Just before 7.30 p.m. the almost empty road began to fill with people, local and visitors. A few people in medieval costume came out of the castle, followed by visiting youth clubs, and mixed with the large crowd, now assembled mostly in front of the doctor's surgery. Four men appeared on top of the high wall adjoining the surgery, carrying two huge baskets. Cheers went up from the crowd, and then for a few moments there was almost complete silence in anticipation of the ceremony. As the donors delved their hands into the baskets, the crowd sprang to life again, with hands outstretched to catch the rain of tiny pieces of bread and cheese descending upon us. Some hit our upturned faces and even penetrated into our pockets, and all the time the crowd was jumping about trying to catch some of the morsels. A young lady next to me caught quite a lot in her upturned skirt, while on the other side a man took off his hat, which by the size of it he had brought with him for the purpose, and caught some in that. The baskets exhausted, the crowd closed the proceedings by clapping and slowly departed, trampling underfoot the carpet of 'manna from heaven'. I asked a collector, who mingled with the crowd collecting contributions, whether the forester's story of thirty years ago still applied today. He looked at me for a moment.

'You must be a stranger,' he said. 'Yes, many people still believe in the power behind these morsels. You keep your fragment in a matchbox. I have three matchboxes from previous years and I wouldn't like to throw them away. I gather this is your first visit, but you must come again.'

A voice from nearby added, 'And don't forget to bring your matchbox. I have mine,' he said, displaying it.

St Briavel (or Brigomaglos) was a hermit who lived in the Forest of Dean in the fifth century. It is interesting to note that the English side of the Wye had its share of Celtic saints as well as the western or Gwent side with its mixed Welsh and English origins.

Above Tintern and on the Gwent side of the Wye is Llandogo, almost on the same parallel as St Briavels. At Llandogo the houses are scattered high up through the woods, which form a wide arc corresponding to a bend of the river. The quay of Llandogo, once busy with the trow trade, no longer exists, although some inn names are reminiscent of the shipping days. The name 'Llandogo' comes from two words: '*llan*' is Welsh for 'church' and appears in many Welsh place-names, followed by the name of a Celtic saint, while '*dogo*' is derived from St Oudoceus, latinized from the Celtic name Euddogwy. He was the third bishop of Llandaff ('church on the River Taff'), Cardiff, and set up a monastery at what is now Llandogo at the end of the sixth century. The pulpit in the church shows St Oudoceus saving a stag from the hounds during a hunt.

St Oudoceus's sympathy with the hunted stag reminds me of a recent incident concerning two anti-hunt ladies who lived in the Devauden area. With similar sentiments to the saint, they set out to confuse the hounds of a hunt by spreading aniseed. Unfortunately, they left their retreat too late and heard the hounds approaching. With the smell of aniseed still on their persons, they fled towards their cottage, with the hounds gaining on them. This time they were the quarry, but they reached home just in time to slam the door and sat there, trying to ignore the frantic yelps of the hounds all around the cottage, mingled with the shouts of the irate huntsmen.

A little to the west of Llandogo is Cleddon with its waterfalls, known as Cleddon Shoots. The Wye Valley Walk passes through Cleddon, a convenient place to follow the nature trails laid out in Cuckoo and Bargain Woods. Cuckoo Wood speaks for itself, but Bargain has also been spelt Bargam. The shoots or falls which form a series of cascades, descending 550 feet in half a mile, can be approached from Llandogo or Tintern or by a less winding road from Trellech. The stream cascades down a ravine just below a junction of lanes with a small car-park from which you can look

The Old Malthouse, Brockweir

down on the upper part of the falls. A footpath leads down along the side of the ravine and, although it seems to lead away from the falls, within a few yards it turns back to a point where a tributary stream crosses it, and here is an excellent viewpoint. Because the approach is through narrow lanes, this is not coach country, so there are not the tourists to be found as at the larger falls of Powis and North Wales. The narrow stream which feeds the falls passes through Cleddon Bog, with its rare plants. Just a short distance along the road from the top of the falls, there is woodland on one side, with glimpses of the yellow surface of the bog between the stunted trees on the other.

The Way to Monmouth

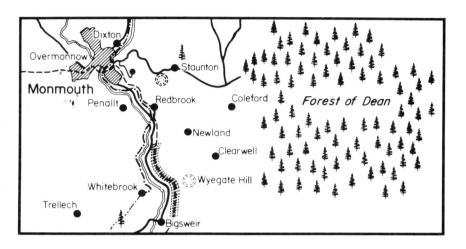

Above Llandogo the main road crosses the river to the eastern side at Bigsweir. Close to the other side of Bigsweir Bridge, a secondary road forks off to the right to join, in about three miles, the B4231 just below Clearwell. Less than three-quarters of a mile from the bridge, this road crosses a well-defined part of Offa's Dyke, which can be followed for quite a distance.

Clearwell gains its name from a spring producing perfectly clear water, and here we find yet another castle. In spite of its medieval appearance, it is an early eighteenth-century house built by Thomas Wyndham about 1727 and believed to be the earliest neo-Gothic house in the country. The usual style of the Georgian period was the neo-classical, but towards the end of the eighteenth century a taste for the medieval became fashionable, so the early date of Clearwell Castle makes it very unusual. It stands on the site of an earlier house, known as Clearwell Court and owned by the Throckmorton family in the early seventeenth century. In fact, the present castle was known as Clearwell Court up to 1908. Thomas Wyndham had his coat of arms carved in the stonework over the courtyard gate and his insignia, the Wyndham lion, carved on the battlements.

Mining machinery at Clearwell

Bigsweir Bridge

In 1663 in the old house was held the first 'Court of Mine Law', set up by the 'free' miners of the Forest of Dean to safeguard their rights and to establish the principles of 'free' mining in the forest. This is not to be confused with the forest laws, which had been established for the royal forests long before to control the taking of venison and other offences.

Caroline, Countess of Dunraven, who died in 1870, a member of the Wyndham family, lived at Clearwell Castle, still then known as Clearwell Court. In 1866 she had the present St Peter's Church built in Clearwell, but pending the building of the church the services were held at the castle. There had been a St Peter's Church on another site, but this was pulled down. She also had the small mortuary chapel built in the old St Peter's churchyard, which is on the right of the road leading up to Clearwell Mine and caves. The churchyard and chapel are known as St Peter's Cemetery and are still used for burials.

There is still in the village a public house, the 'Wyndham Arms', which is sixteenth- to seventeenth-century.

Since the time of building, there have been various alterations and additions to Clearwell Castle, and in 1929 a fire destroyed some of the interior. The building continued to deteriorate, but after the war it was acquired by a Mr Yeats, who had been born there and who had always wanted to come back and make his home there. Yeats and his family worked very hard to repair and restore the castle and opened it to the public. It is now owned by Mr and Mrs Russell Steele and their daughter, who have converted it into a charming country hotel and restaurant, with very attractive gardens complete with peacocks. There were about eighteen of these at the time of my last visit. It is open on Sundays, and sometimes guided tours are arranged. Much of the eighteenth-century interior has gone, but it has been well restored and some of the original fireplaces remain. In the banqueting hall a complete history of the Wyndham family is displayed on the wall.

A feature of Clearwell is the old ironmine, now open to the public, one of many mines once worked in the forest. Many now remain abandoned as holes in the ground, and there are in places opencast workings now forming complicated systems of shallow gorges, known as 'scowles', such as those just west of Coleford, known as 'Puzzle Wood'.

The Clearwell mine is not of the opencast variety but is partly natural cave and partly worked rock, entered by a short passage or adit. Although the floor inside slopes down, there are no difficult gradients, and the paths are well beaten and illuminated. At various points descriptive notices have been set up, and various objects used in mining days are exhibited. The chambers in the mine are large and lofty and in mining language are known as 'churns'. There are six, all inter-connecting, at Clearwell, originally formed by the scouring and solvent action of water. Such chambers sometimes become filled or partly filled by mineral deposits, such as iron ore, as at Clearwell.

The Clearwell mine is owned by Mr Ray Wright, and he and his son Jonathan have in recent years carried out many improvements, making the mine easy for public tours; like the castle, it is a popular attraction in Clearwell. Mr Wright is himself a 'free' miner and has served for some years as secretary of the Royal Forest of Dean Free Miners' Association. A free miner is one who has the right to work minerals in the Forest of Dean and is registered as a free miner. This privilege is not acquired by examination but by birthright. The origin of the custom is unknown, but Edward I certainly gave it his royal blessing in appreciation of the assistance given to him by the inhabitants of the Hundreds of St Briavels during his wars against Wales and Scotland. He had the rights of the free miners codified in a

Clearwell Castle

document which was to become known as the 'Book of Dennis'. The origin of the name 'Dennis' is unknown but may well have been derived from 'Denu' a Celtic word for a wood or forest. This is thought to be the origin of the present name of the Forest of Dean.

In the *Book of Dennis* it is laid down that to become a free miner it was necessary to have been born in the Hundred of St Briavels and to have worked as a miner, under a free miner, for a year and a day. Then the applicant was qualified to register as a free miner with the gaveller, the King's agent. In recent years, expectant mothers of the Forest have often been sent to the maternity hospital in Gloucester, and so their children are born out of the Hundred and cannot become free miners, so that there is a move to establish a local maternity unit.

Mining is not the only right: there are also rights of free grazing, and these sometimes led to friction with newcomers who settled in the Forest and complained that sheep had invaded their gardens and eaten their produce. Naturally those who own the rights guard them jealously, and those who settle in the area should respect them. The answer may well be a good fence and a shut gate.

Iron has been worked in the forest since Roman times, but it is not the only mineral mined there. For many years free miners have worked coal by individual pits, usually by tunnelling into the hillside, either as a one-man project or in partnership with one or two other free miners. Most of these have now disappeared, but there are still a few of these small mines. The longest surviving and most productive product of the forest is not mineral but timber, much of which is under the control of the Forestry Commission.

On the west bank of the Wye is Whitebrook, once an industrial valley but now a haven of rural beauty. The way from the forest is back over Bigsweir Bridge and then north along the western side of the Wye to Tump Farm. This building may have been a custom house connected with the river trade, together with Wyeseal Farm on the eastern side of the river.

The lane turns west and travels up a valley overlooking a stream. This is the White Brook which has cut its valley deep in places, well below the level of the road. The steep sides are well covered by a variety of deciduous trees and occasionally conifers, these at a little higher level. As we ascend the valley, we pass at intervals pleasant houses and old ivy-covered ruins of ancient mills and furnaces. Some of the houses were once millhouses, sometimes three storeys high, and the millponds have been converted to garden features, some as sunken gardens, some kept as decorative garden ponds,

In 1606 wireworks were established at Whitebrook to take surplus orders which the works established at Tintern since 1556 could not meet. The wiremaking industry in the area was first established at Tintern, with imported German technicians and labour, a move by the Government to establish this industry to discourage the importing of wire from abroad. Both the Tintern and the Whitebrook works were driven by water-power. An early process was the manufacture of iron bars at the forge using selected ores from the surrounding district. These were then flattened into plates by water-powered heavy hammers, cut into strips and rounded by rollers into coarse wire.

Later it was possible, by introducing further German expertise, to make thin wire by the wire-drawing process. This method involved the making of a more tensile metal, iron first being chosen from Lydbrook. Iron rods, made in the local forges, were heated, elongated and annealed and submerged in water for several weeks. They were then cut into suitable lengths, rounded by hammering and drawn mechanically through a suitably sized tapered hole in a metal plate, according to the gauge of wire required.

Whitebrook as it is today probably first came into being with the establishment there of the German community who came to work in the wireworks. These works closed about 1720.

About 1760 papermills were established at Whitebrook. There were five or six of them, all dependent on the waters of the White Brook. They came under a series of owners up to and in the nineteenth century, with names such as Clearwater, The Glyn, Wye Valley, Sunnyside and Ferndale. Banknote paper was among the products, although not for the Bank of England.

A few miles north of Whitebrook is Penallt, an apt Welsh name – '*pen*' means 'top' and '*allt*' 'hillside' – for here Penallt village climbs the slope of the hill. The largest house, the Argoed, was a favourite rendezvous of the early Fabian Socialists, and here George Bernard Shaw wrote to Ellen Terry in glowing terms about the beauty of the area.

The old church stands in isolation away from the scattering of modern houses which creep up the Penallt hillside. Surrounded by its ancient churchyard, with wonderful views across the Wye to the hills beyond, it has an air of remoteness seemingly far removed from the modern world, and indeed, although the old church is still used for services, a new church was erected in 1869 as a chapel of ease for the convenience of the parishioners, down the hill among the older houses. Although the interior was restored in 1887, the structure still contains much of genuine antiquity, such as the tower and chancel arch. The oldest item is the massive oak church chest made out of a solid piece of oak, believed to date from the twelfth century. The village stocks and whipping-post once stood outside the lychgate, and the huge stone nearby may have been used as a mounting-block for parishioners arriving on horseback and perhaps as a coffin rest before entering the church. Not far away is a curiously named oak tree, 'Vermin Oak', where the last wild boar in Wales is said to have been killed.

From the church, a steep hill runs down towards the Wye, and by the Boat Inn the Wye Valley Walk crosses the river by a footway adjoining an old iron railway bridge to Redbrook, situated on both the Offa's Dyke Walk and the Wye Valley Walk. It consists of two villages, Upper and Lower Redbrook, and was concerned with the iron industry, not for the mining of iron, for this was done on the limestone plateau, but it had the water-power to drive the mills for the smelting and forging of iron. The first ironworks was set up in Upper Redbrook during the first few years of the seventeenth century, and some thirty years later another appeared nearer the river. The second works closed down about 1725, but a new works was established on or near the same site and lasted until 1816.

Redbrook had also other industries, such as copper-smelting, in spite of the fact that, apart from a few traces of malachite, to be seen as almost invisible green specks in many limestone areas, it possessed no copper ore worth smelting and depended on Cornwall for its supply of ore. As brass is a mixture of copper and zinc, the lack of local ore may have been one of the reasons why the brass wire industry at Tintern was not so long-lived as the iron. However, the copperworks at Redbrook are known to have lasted for some forty years, from about 1692 to 1730, although Rudder wrote in 1779 as if the two copperworks and an iron furnace at Redbrook were still in existence.

There is a possibility that the copper-smelting at Redbrook was started in 1692 in the belief that copper ore was available within the district. One of the Swedish copper experts who came over to advise on the copper-smelting, Eric Odelstierna, wrote in that year that the company had been mining in the Forest of Dean and had smelted a small amount of copper. However, it was probably a small pocket, for Thomas Gletscher reported, six years later, that the Forest supply had been exhausted. Some fifty tons of Cornish ore arrived at Chepstow in 1691, presumably for use in the new copperworks at Redbrook, so it does not appear that the company was relying on the local source. Had there been ample local supplies of ore, the copper industry at Redbrook would probably have lasted longer, for wood (for charcoal) and coal were readily available locally. At the time of the establishment of the Redbrook works, the Cornish copper-mining industry was being revived. In fact, there was a connection between the two areas, as John Coster, who is buried in Newland church, contributed to the development of the Redbrook works and was also involved in mining in Cornwall.

Andrew Green in *Our Haunted Kingdom*, published in 1973, relates a fascinating story of hauntings near Redbrook at the Swan Pool. There is quite a collection of wraiths. A tall woman in white, draped with dripping weed and with a moaning child in her arms, is reputed to have been seen rising slowly from the water. A baby crying has been heard from afar. A black dog, sometimes described as headless, comes from a limekiln in the nearby woods and turns back to the kiln, after running round the Swan Pool. It is said that all three were murdered at the same time. The pool is in Swanpool Wood and adjoins the left-hand side of the road from Newland, less than a mile from and due east of Upper Redbrook. In size it is more a lake than a pool, and at one end a railed dam is accessible from the road. Green scum on the water and encroaching overground woodland give it a complete air of abandonment. No wonder it has its ghost story.

To the east of Redbrook is Newland. The village dates from about 1219, when it was founded by Robert de Wakering, who cleared a part of the Dean Forest for the purpose, so it was indeed a 'new land'. The church of All Saints is imposing and spacious and is aptly known as 'the Cathedral of the Forest'. It has a fine collection of monuments, including one to Jenkyn or Jun (John) Wyrall, a forester of the Royal Forest. It is dated to 1457 and depicts the forester in hunting dress, complete with his horn, knife and sword. The forester's effigy on the quatrefoiled decorated tomb chest was once outside the church but was moved into the building to protect it from the weather. Tombs of the nobility in

All Saints church, Newland

their armour and of the clergy in their robes are common enough in British churches, but it is indeed a rarity to see such an elaborate tomb belonging to a commoner – and a forester at that, depicted with all the tools of his calling and in his woodland dress in which he patrolled the forest looking for game and poachers. He seems more real and human than the armoured knights.

Here, too, we find a stone slab from a tomb inscribed with the figure of a bowman, with bow, dagger and horn. Was he one of the archers who accompanied the king on his hunting trips, perhaps as a huntsman, but perhaps also as a bodyguard? Although the stone bears no inscription or date, as does the Wyrall tomb, the dress dates it to the early seventeenth century. We do not know the bowman's name, nor those of the two clergy in simple priestly robes, one of the thirteenth century and the other of the later half of the fourteenth century, who are depicted on other tomb slabs in the church.

The figure which is better known, because it has been reproduced many times in literature about the forest, is that of the miner. It is a small brass inserted on a tomb slab to which it does not appear to belong. The miner, his pick raised in his right hand, is dressed in belted tunic, with his trousers tied with thongs below the knees, a cap to protect his head and a hod on his back. He is

The Ostrich Hotel, Newland

The almshouses and cross at Newland

clearly at work, and in his mouth is a holder with a candle to provide light and yet leave his hands free. There cannot be many of these miners' hods, or 'butties', used for carrying the products of their work on their backs.

Nobody knows the origin of the miner's brass at Newland. It has been suggested that it represents a crest and the figure of the miner is shown above a helmet, but what knight would carry such a device? Others say that the miner is shown above the helmet to indicate that the miners' rights superseded that of the feudal lords. However, one would not expect a miner to have a brass memorial, and so the miner's brass remains a mystery.

There are also traditional types of tomb effigies in Newland church, such as those of Sir John and Lady Joce, who died in 1344 (or 1349) and 1362. The effigies were re-cut in 1862, and the side panels replaced. If the miner's brass is a copy of an unusual crest, so is that of Sir John Joce, for his head rests on a stone helm crested with a bearded Saracen's head, more appropriate to a knight and perhaps inherited from an illustrious ancestor of the Crusader days. His lady wears the square headdress of the period.

As this was a forest church, there was once a chantry priest here
who performed Morowe services. Twice a week he went from
mine to mine and from smithy to smithy to say Mass for those
unable to attend church because of their work.

Newland was fortunate in having two rectors of wealth and
influence, who added to the building of the church. In 1247 the
rector was Walter Giffard, who became Bishop of Bath and Wells
in 1264, Chancellor of England in 1265 and Archbishop of York in
1266, when his brother Geoffrey succeeded him as Chancellor.
Geoffrey later became Bishop of Worcester and in 1272 chief
regent of the kingdom. Walter was succeeded as Rector of Newland by a monk from Westminster known as John of London and
called 'the Beaver', presumably because he delved so industri-
ously into Church and State matters. Among other activities he
became Edward I's historian.

Some years ago the churchyard was tidied up. Some of the
headstones were moved to one side and others covered over. The
surface was seeded with grass to make a large, easily maintained
area, except for the cross and table tombs. In 1985 it was decided
to remove the grass in places to reveal the old inscribed tomb slabs
to help augment the church burial records.

Near the churchyard are the old grammar school of 1639, which
bears the arms of Edward Bell, and the 1615 almshouses established by William Jones, a year after he had endowed Monmouth
School. Once when I was reading the plaque on the front of the
almshouse, a man's head appeared at the open window above.
'Why don't you come in?' he said, 'and see the inside'. I had been
in his apartment for only a few minutes when his conversation
turned to other matters. 'I would offer you a bottle of beer and
usually I have a couple of bottles here, but unfortunately I am
completely out.'

I took the hint and walked over to the early eighteenth-century
local, 'the Ostrich', and asked for two bottles of beer.

'What kind do you want?' I was asked.

'I don't know. They're not for me – they're for –'

'So you've been visiting the almshouses,' said the landlord,
putting two bottles on the counter.

When I got back to the almshouses, my friend was waiting at
the open door. He took the bottles and closed the door and I went
on my way to Monmouth, where William Jones, the founder of
the Newland Almshouses, also endowed Monmouth School in
1614.

The old Grammar School, Newland

The centre of Monmouth is Agincourt Square, so named because Henry V, the victor of Agincourt, was born in Monmouth Castle in 1387. Just a few ruins of wall and the lower part of a tower are all that is left of the castle, which is approached by Castle Hill from Agincourt Square. In the square, a rather ugly, squat figure of Henry V, on a pedestal in a niche high up in the façade of the 1724 Shire Hall, looks down on the more attractive statue of C. S. Rolls, another local celebrity and the founder of Rolls Royce Ltd, holding a model of an aeroplane. He was killed in a flying accident in 1910.

Another local notable was Geoffrey of Monmouth, on whose spurious history many of England's earlier kings based their pedigrees; also many of the later romantic tales of the Arthurian legends originated in his stories. He was probably a monk of the Benedictine priory at Monmouth; what is left of it is incorporated into a building now used as a youth hostel, but he never looked out from that first-floor castellated bay window known as 'Geoffrey's Window', facing Priory Street, for it is late fifteenth-century and he died in 1154. Still, it is the most photographed window in Monmouth.

The Local History Centre and Museum, which share a common entrance vestibule with the post office in the Market Hall in Priory Street, contain a considerable collection of Nelson relics. However, the town has no connection with the Admiral except for

Geoffrey's Window, Monmouth

two visits which included a journey along the Wye and a stay
at the eighteenth-century coaching inn, the Beaufort Arms, in
Agincourt Square. Nelson breakfasted with certain of the local
dignitaries on the Kymin overlooking the town. The extensive
collection of relics was made by Lady Llangattock, who died in
1923, leaving them to Monmouth, together with items belonging
to her family.

Monmouth is certainly a town of ancient inns and has had

many famous visitors. Wordsworth stayed at the Beaufort Arms in Agincourt Square, where, in fine weather, you can eat and drink in Continental fashion in the courtyard, once a fives court, and view passers-by through the old coaching arch. Cromwell rested at the Queen's Head, a timber-framed old coaching inn, over 350 years old. Some old inns have disappeared. 'The Royal George', built in 1737, is now the name of a site developed for twenty flats. The Free Institute for Working Men, which proudly

The Shire Hall, Monmouth

displays a tablet stating that it was founded and endowed by Mrs Matilda Jones in 1866, now houses a picture-frame business.

Some of the large houses, particularly those near Monmouth School, have changed their use. The Grange, which still displays an old insurance fireplate, houses Monmouth Preparatory School, and further on St James's House is now its junior school. Here an attempt is said to have been made on Cromwell's life by a Royalist named Evans, but this story may not be true. One version says that the attempt took place in the Queen's Head and that the ghost of the assailant still haunts the inn. Opposite St James's House is a catalpa or Indian Bean tree, which blooms during July. Although Monmouth School was founded in 1614, most of the subsidiary houses are older than the main buildings, as the school was much enlarged during the last half of the nineteenth century.

Monnow Street, the main shopping thoroughfare, connects Agincourt Square with the thirteenth-century Monnow Bridge, with its protective gate guarding the crossing of the Monnow and probably once used as a tollhouse. The river here is the Monnow, or the Little Wye, which joins the main River Wye at Monmouth – hence the town's name, the mouth or junction of the Monnow. There are no other military fortified bridges in Britain, except castle moat bridges, and the Monnow Gate is certainly a highlight of any historian's visit to Gwent. It was a protection for the bridge and not a town gate, for the town gates have all disappeared, although the edge of the east gate still remains built into the corner of a house in Lower Dixton Road. The loopholes on the west face were made in anticipation of a Chartists' attack in 1839, while the pedestrian doorways were a later nineteenth-century addition, in the interests of road safety when the road was widened.

St Mary's Church is not outstanding except for the spire, conspicuous as you approach Monmouth from the north and, like that at Ross, a good landmark. The main body of the church was rebuilt in 1881. Among the fragments from the earlier church on the site is a cresset stone which was an early means of lighting, having a number of hollows in which wax or oil was burnt – a rare survival, but there is an excellent one in Brecon Cathedral, and I was lucky to find a fragment of one on my own site at Keynsham while excavating with my own team of helpers on the site of Keynsham Abbey, Avon, part way between Bristol and Bath. Only two or three of the egg cup shaped hollows survived but enough to gladden the heart of any director of archaeological excavations, always with the hope that more of it will be found. Some fourteenth-century tiles there are of the same date as some at St Mary's.

There is a large parking area on the town side of Monnow Bridge, behind the buildings in Monnow Street. It incorporates the cattle market and is part of the large meadow known as Chippenham Mead, a recreation area. The name is derived from the Old English *ceapian*, meaning to buy, and hence a market, as in the Wiltshire Chippenham and in the Avon Chipping Sodbury. An open space in Tetbury, now used as a car-park, is known as 'The Chippings', its name derived from the same source.

Today the open general market is restricted to Agincourt Square under the colonnade of the Shire Hall by the entrance to the magistrates' courts. Here you can buy practically anything,

Monnow Bridge and Gate, Monmouth

including clothes, jewellery, kitchenware and second-hand books. Before Monnow Street was built, the old market spread onto a meadow between Agincourt Square and the westerly town gate, known as St Stephen's Gate.

It is interesting that the once-garrisoned castle still has military connections, for Great Castle House, adjoining the ruins, is now occupied by the Royal Monmouthshire Royal Engineers (Militia) Supplementary Reserve. The house was purchased by the War Department about 1875 from the previous owner, the Duke of Beaufort. The central part of the house was built in 1673, probably using stone from the castle ruins. The wings were added in the early twentieth century. The third Marquis of Worcester, who later became the first Duke of Beaufort, built the house, it is said, so that his grandchild could be born adjacent to Henry V's birthplace. The building, which has outstanding plasterwork, is open to the public only at certain times.

Overmonnow, now part of Monmouth, was originally a separate town, and tradition has it that in medieval times it was known as 'Cappers' Town', associated with the making of Monmouth caps, although there is no real evidence for this belief. The Monmouth caps were close-fitting, round and made of wool. Shakespeare mentions them in his *Henry V*, when Fluellen says that the Welshmen were 'wearing leeks in their Monmouth caps'. The industry came to an end through a disastrous plague, when it apparently moved to Bewdley.

Two miles out of Monmouth and off the Staunton Road is the Kymin, a hill with extensive views of the town. It is a curious name believed to have derived from the Welsh *cae maen*, field of stone. Whether you go by the more direct route by Shanks's pony or by car up the steep, winding lane, it is quite a climb. It is a lengthy, narrow lane with steep gradients and sharp bends and can be quite alarming when you meet a car coming down, but a picturesque route, mostly between trees, with glimpses of isolated houses. The town of Monmouth grows smaller as the road climbs higher and higher. At last a swing to the left brings you into a spacious earthen car-park, provided by the National Trust. A couple of minutes walk and you are on the summit, 840 feet high.

From the Kymin, wooded hills can be seen all around, and the river far below looks little more than a brook. On a neighbouring hill you catch a glimpse of a white house, and on the Kymin itself there are houses almost to the summit. You are amazed at the height at which the local people built their houses around Monmouth, but who can blame them with such a panorama? I met a lady who lived just below the summit. Her grandchildren were playing on the old bowling green and I asked how children who lived at such a height managed to get to and from school. She told me that there were several children living high on the hill, enough to justify a school mini-bus.

On the summit is the white castellated eighteenth-century Round House, now the residence of the National Trust agent and his family. The house has a viewing terrace on the side overlooking the town and a small cannon on the other side, pointing skywards. Why a house in this exposed and, in those days, isolated position? Philip Meakins Hardwick and a group of wealthy Monmouth gentlemen had it built as a summer house in 1793–4, where they could retire from the crowds of the town and hold their meetings and dining parties in rural seclusion. There was even the bowling green where the children were playing, and you can still see the flat surface at a slightly lower level behind the house. It must have been an arduous task cutting it into the irregular hillside and banking it up on its far side, which stands higher than the slope of the hill and is bounded by a stone wall. No doubt, at that time, there was ample estate labour for the work.

Close to the Round House is the Naval Temple, built of two deep alcoves back-to-back with bench seats and with seating along the outside of the two flank walls, shaded by pent roofs. The pyramid roof of the central part of the building is surmounted by an arched structure, forming a pedestal for a figure of Britannia. This structure and the walls above the pent roof are adorned with medallions, each inscribed with the names of British admirals and their principal battles from 1759 to 1801, sixteen of them, including Nelson. The temple was erected on 1 August 1800 to commemorate Nelson's victory at the Battle of the Nile on the

The Kymin, Monmouth

The Round House, the Kymin, Monmouth

same date two years earlier. The inscription on the wall of the temple reads as follows:

This NAVAL TEMPLE
was erected August 1st 1800
to perpetuate the names of those
Noble Admirals
who distinguished themselves by their
GLORIOUS VICTORIES FOR ENGLAND
in the last and present wars
and is respectfully dedicated to
HER GRACE the DUTCHESS OF BEAUFORT

(The 't' in 'Dutchess' is not a printer's error.)

Boscawen is one of the admirals whose name is on the temple with the date 18 August 1759, when he pursued the French fleet, captured three of its large ships, burnt two and took 2,000 prisoners. This action destroyed the French chances of basing their fleet at Brest for their proposed invasion of England. The other vessels concentrated at Brest were defeated off Quiberon by Hawke on 20 November in the same year, as recorded on one of the medallions. The other admirals named on the Temple were involved in later battles in the eighteenth and early nineteenth centuries. The summit of the Kymin and its buildings were acquired by public subscription and transferred to the National Trust in 1902, one hundred years from Nelson's visit, when he breakfasted at the Round House and visited the Temple.

Dixton, on the north-eastern edge of Monmouth, was originally approached directly by Dixton Road but is now separated from Monmouth by the dual carriageway. St Peter's Church is a small, quaint building, with a churchyard extending to the bank of the River Wye, where steps mark the site of the old ferry which has not operated for many years. Because of its nearness to the river, the church has suffered from flooding at times, and tablets within the church indicate the amazingly high flood levels.

The church was originally dedicated to Didwg, probably a Celtic missionary, but was re-dedicated to St Peter, Tydiuc, in Norman times. In the middle of the thirteenth century it was known as St Peter's Diuc'ston, and finally in the fifteenth century spelt as Dixton. It was probably one of the buildings destroyed by Gruffydd ap Llywelyn, for it was rebuilt about 1080, when it was placed in the charge of the Benedictines, who had their priory in Monmouth until the Dissolution, when a lay rector was appointed. As a border church, its jurisdiction has swung between England and Wales. Firstly it was appropriated from the Welsh Church about 1100 by the Bishop of Hereford, to return to the diocese of Llandaff in the nineteenth century. In 1914 certain border parishes were allowed to choose whether to come under English or Welsh jurisdiction, and Dixton chose to return to Hereford and still remains within the Deanery of Archenfield and the Hereford diocese.

There are two rare objects within the church. One the visitor can see is the Queen Anne coat of arms, the other he cannot see as it is hung in the belfry: a bell with the inscribed heads of Edward III and Philippa his queen, forming the stops in the inscription. Such Royal Head bells are certainly rare, and this one is thought to have been cast about 1420, some forty years after Edward's death.

The church itself is long and narrow, with some very attractive modern glass. The tower and a large part of the existing building are of thirteenth-century origin, but some restoration was carried out in Victorian times, and in 1860 the old porch was replaced and removed to Dixton cottage, a picturesque building adjoining the gate to the church. It is more the size of a farmhouse then a

St Peter's church, Dixton

cottage and was once the rectory. This old house is at the end of the lane from the dual carriageway and, with the church bordering the Wye, seems to be in another place and time from the hurried world rushing past a few hundred yards away.

7

Up the Monnow

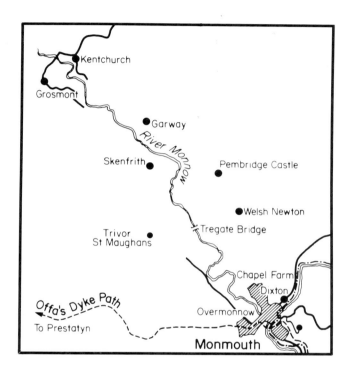

Back across the dual carriageway we are in Monmouth, lying in a peninsula between the Wye flowing from the north-east and its tributary the Monnow, or Little Wye, flowing from the north-west.

Some six miles or so up the Monnow valley is Skenfrith, where the castle, mill, unusual-looking church and inn make an attractive centre of the village. Skenfrith Castle, which has the Welsh name of Castell Ynysgynwraidd (tongue-twisting to anyone but a Welshman), is now a mere shell but was once quite a formidable fortress. It was one of the three border castles which defended the route from Hereford into Wales and protected the border against the Welsh raiders. The other two were Grosmont and White Castle, four to five miles away in opposite directions. The three

Skenfrith Castle

castles formed an important defensive triangle, and their lord was always somebody whom the king considered trustworthy.

Immediately following the Conquest, William I divided the land between his Norman supporters, who not only defended their area but provided manpower for further conquest. Locally he appointed William fitz Osbern, whom he made Earl of Hereford. The first castles erected would have been of the type known as motte-and-bailey structures. The motte was an artificial hillock on which a wooden keep was built, later to be replaced by a stone keep, surrounded by the bailey, an area containing the domestic buildings, all enclosed by a pale fence, replaced in due course by a perimeter or curtain wall, protected at corners and other convenient points by towers or bastions.

Skenfrith was constructed in the early thirteenth century, with a keep and a curtain wall, with towers at each of its four corners. Later a fifth tower was added between the south-western and north-western towers. These are all in various stages of dilapidation, especially the north-western tower, where only the semicircular foundations can be seen. The motte-and-bailey origin of the castle is clear from the position of the keep and the original bailey area. The curtain walls still rise to an appreciable height, although the gatehouse has gone.

The church is dedicated to St Bridget, an Irish saint of a charitable nature. One legend says that she cut up the bishop's fine vestments to clothe the poor, another that she gave away so many of her father's possessions that he gave her away to the King of Ulster, who helped her to set up a priory at Kildare. The church was built early in the thirteenth century close to the castle and, in fact, was the garrison church. It was probably Hubert de Burgh who rebuilt the castle in stone and built the church, as he was both incumbent and lord of the manor at the time. He later became Chief Justiciar under Henry III. Quite a lot of the original structure remains, but much of the internal furnishing is Jacobean. One of its proudest possessions is the fifteenth-century cope displayed in a glass wall case. No important alterations were made to the structure between 1663 and 1909, so the church escaped the drastic facelifts applied to many churches during the nineteenth century.

One of the most fascinating features of the exterior of the church is the squat tower with its pyramid roof which not only accommodated the bells but was also a dovecote. Pigeon pie was no doubt a welcome addition to the garrison's winter menu, but

many of the old church towers in this border country were refuges
for the parishioners during raids or battles, and it was hard to
provide ready sustenance for the incarcerated villagers when it
was impossible to get food supplies through. A gate just beyond
the castle leads into a meadow, and you can walk to the weir and
the millrace which runs beside the castle. A walk along the outside
of the castle curtain wall will bring you to a doorway where steps
lead up to the bailey. Further along at the end of the wall can be
seen the mill and its waterwheel.

Some five miles from Skenfrith further up the Monnow is the
sister castle of Grosmont, now a ruin but once perhaps the most
important of the three castles. The first record of the castle was in
1162, but Gwent fell to the Normans in 1067–75 so it is likely that
there was a Norman timber castle before the twelfth century.
King John gave the castles to Hubert de Burgh, but when he was
captured and imprisoned in France, the King transferred them to
William de Braose, the Lord of Abergavenny. However, in 1208
de Braose fell out of favour and fled to France, and for a brief
period the castles were held by John of Monmouth. After King
John's death, de Burgh regained possession of the three castles in
1218 and rebuilt Grosmont to the plan we see today, in the typical
military style of the early thirteenth century, distinguished by
projecting circular towers from which the archers could cover the
connecting walls against attack.

Hubert de Burgh had a chequered career under Henry III and
lost and regained the King's favour and his castles several times.
Once, in 1233, when Henry was staying at Grosmont Castle, one
of Hubert's supporters attacked the castle at night and the King's
sleeping army were taken by surprise and had to flee in their
nightclothes. Eventually the three castles were granted to Prince
Edward, later to become Edward I, and then to his younger
brother, the Earl of Lancaster.

The Welsh leader Owain Glyndwr led a rising against Gwent
and attacked Grosmont but was defeated. In the following year,
1404, his son Gruffydd led another unsuccessful attack, which
was the beginning of the end of Welsh resistance. The castle was
eventually allowed to fall into disrepair and was in a ruinous state
by the middle of the sixteenth century.

Grosmont church is dedicated to St Nicholas of Myra, a
favourite saint of the Normans, and this would indicate that there
was probably a settlement, with church and castle, established in
Norman times. It is believed that the church was rebuilt by

Grosmont Castle

Hubert de Burgh, at the same time as the castle, in the early thirteenth century. Like the Skenfrith church, St Nicholas's was a garrison church. It is now too large for the needs of the village and is divided by a screen. One part is used as the present church and has been well restored; the remainder, known as 'the old nave', is cold and empty, its stone floor paved with ledger slabs, mostly of the eighteenth and early nineteenth centuries. It has the appearance of a large barn for there is an old haycart in one corner and several agricultural implements in another. However, both parts of the church are of considerable architectural interest. The restored part is very much a living church, a pleasant mixture of Early English and late Victorian restoration, while the old nave is now virtually a museumpiece with still the austere simplicity of an early church. It is rare to find such a contrast within the same building.

Before 1880 the church was in poor structural condition. Large cracks had developed, and to save the structure, extensive restoration was necessary. The tower was unstable and the whole area below was excavated down to solid rock and filled with concrete, while much of the supporting structure was rebuilt. During the restoration, the present east window was inserted, together with the screen separating the church from the old nave. The octagonal font with Norman cable decoration, which once stood by the entrance to the old nave, was moved into the part of the church now used for worship. This part still retains some of its thirteenth-century features, including a row of seven windows on the south side, the thirteenth-century double piscina and four crux arches. There were galleries for musicians and singers, but these were taken down during the restoration of the church.

An effigy in the church is said to be that of John of Kent, a fourteenth-century wizard alleged to have been buried in the wall of the church to cheat the Devil. In return for granting him occult powers, the Devil was to take possession of his soul at death, whether he was buried inside or outside the church. This story is not unique either to Grosmont or to John of Kent, as Winterbourne church, near Bristol, has a similar tale. There are many stories of the magical powers and mystic lore of John of Kent. He is said to have been born in Pembrokeshire and as a boy to have been a servant at Kentchurch Court, just across the river from Grosmont. One of his jobs was to scare the crows off the crops, and the story goes that he could 'freeze' them in a barn while he took time off to visit Grosmont fair. He even had a contest in stone-throwing with the Devil, and the standing stones at Trellech were said to have been the result. Grosmont was a lively town, and John of Kent must have been fond of visiting it, as he is said, through his unholy powers, to have built a bridge across the Monnow between Grosmont and Kentchurch. Even today the Bridge Inn has a sign showing a dancing devil.

Whatever the legends, John of Kent, if indeed there really was such a person, was probably a priest of Kentchurch, well known for his learning and dabbling into the mysteries of science. He was believed to have been educated by the Franciscans and to have become a Franciscan priest. The local people must have regarded his strange learning with awe and misgiving, and it is said that there was a saying in the district: 'as clever as the Devil or as John of Kent'.

Another colourful personality connected with Kentchurch is Owain Glyndwr, the Welsh leader, who devastated the region at the beginning of the fifteenth century. Indeed, there is a legend that John of Kent was none other than Glyndwr himself, whose end is shrouded in mystery. After his final defeat, he was said to have gone into hiding and lived with one of his daughters. A daughter had married into the Scudamore family of Kentchurch Court and, although two other places claim the honour, he may well have ended his days there.

Cross the bridge built by John of Kent's sorcery to visit Kentchurch Court, originally a fourteenth-century fortified house, on the site of an earlier building. The two medieval parts and chapel were partly rebuilt by Nash about 1800, refaced in a Georgian style and connected by additional rooms and a porch. You can still see the fortified gateway and the medieval tower, which Nash increased in height and the great hall. There is a fifteenth-century Flemish painting, a curious portrait of a grim, sharp-featured man with the old mansion in the background, thought to be the earliest painting of a manor house in the country. The portrait is reputed to be that of John of Kent, and the piercing eye and intensity of expression certainly suggest unusual powers of personality. 'Owain Glyndwr's chamber' is in the medieval tower, quite a pleasant room with the original stairs now blocked off in an alcove.

There are some fine plaster ceilings in the house, but perhaps its greatest treasures are the magnificent wood-carvings by Grinling Gibbons, which came from another house of the Scudamores, Holme Lacy. These clusters of carved fruit, leaves, birds and

St Nicholas's church, Grosmont

flowers adorn several mantelpieces, and on the high wall of the chapel are two exceptionally large carvings in oak which were on the outside of the house at Holme Lacy. Another connection with this house is a portrait of John Scudamore, who lived at Holme Lacy and introduced the red streak cider apple and the Hereford cattle. There are many other fine portraits of the family. Mrs Scudamore, the owner, also shows the staining on the drawing-room wallpaper, caused by severe flooding in the 1950s, when the water poured through the house several feet deep. The extent of the disaster was evident from various photographs taken at that time. Outside the house, on rising ground, is a great herd of fallow deer, culled annually to keep the numbers in a proper ratio to the available pasture. The carcases are sold as venison.

Through Kentchurch a road leads back along the Hereford side of the Monnow towards Skenfrith, passing through Garway, a straggling village with the strangest of churches. In the latter part of the twelfth century, Garway was given to the Order of the Knights Templars, a religious order originally established to guard the pilgrim routes to the Holy Land. The Templars built round churches after the shape of the Holy Sepulchre in Jerusalem. The arc of the circular foundation of the church they built at Garway, excavated in the 1920s, protrudes from underneath the later nave, creating a bizarre effect. The heavy detached early thirteenth-century tower, set at a peculiar angle to the nave, is almost like a castle keep, grim and cheerless, with narrow slit windows. It conjures up visions of warrior knights bearing the cross on their surcoats, protecting pilgrims on the way to Jerusalem, but probably as ruthless as the Saracens. It was linked to the nave in the seventeenth century by a short corridor, leading to the fine interior. There is the magnificent chancel arch with its typical Norman zigzag decoration, a relic of the earlier round Templar church. The columns supporting the arch are surmounted by capitals with Norman decoration, the waterleaf typical of the late twelfth century and a grotesque face or mask, its chin covered with what has been described as a stream of water but which appears to be a beard. The beaded ribbon pattern on both sides of the face is reminiscent of Saxon Romanesque work. Adjoining the chancel arch is a thirteenth-century side chapel with a separate entrance from outside. It is believed to have been the Templars' initiation chapel.

After the Templars were disbanded in 1308, the estate was granted to the Knights Hospitallers, who built the *columbarium* (dovecote), the circular building to be seen in the adjoining farmyard. A Latin inscription says it was built in 1326.

From Garway a lane skirting the Monnow leads south to Skenfrith and continues along the river valley to St Maughans, passing a house called Trivor, an old farmhouse with priests' holes and a secret chapel. The family living there in the seventeenth century were in trouble for sheltering a Roman Catholic priest. St Maughans is a scattered hamlet, and its church is hard to find at the end of a narrow lane, said to have been the highway from Monmouth to Grosmont, then a fair-sized town. The church may date back to Saxon times, although it seems to have been rebuilt or restored several times. The font is believed to be Saxon of the ninth or tenth century. A curious feature is an arcade of oak-tree trunks which replaced a stone arcade, probably of the early thirteenth century. The church and indeed the whole area suffered from Owain Glyndwr's rebellion, and this wooden arcade may have replaced the stone when the church was restored. Another reconstruction was carried out by the grandfather of C. S. Rolls, of Rolls-Royce fame, when the wooden pillars were covered with matchboarding, presumably because they were too rustic, the old box pews were removed and the floor was levelled using old memorial stones. The church pamphlet says that the matchboarding was removed in 1935 by the curate, who borrowed a poker for this purpose from a neighbouring farm. The district was known to have several Roman Catholic families, and so St Maughans was a favourite church for furtive burials according to the banned Catholic rites, and some of the memorials bear symbols of the old religion, the Sacred Heart and the letters IHS.

A lane leads to the main Skenfrith to Monmouth Road, but you can get to Monmouth by crossing the Monnow by the Tregate bridge and following southwards a narrow, twisting lane close to the east bank of the river, with superb views of the valley. However, across the bridge another extremely steep and narrow lane leads eastwards to Welsh Newton. This remote part of the Monnow valley must have been a hidden centre of the old religion, for just before Welsh Newton the lane passes a house called Cwm, rebuilt in Georgian style in the early nineteenth century. The old house was the secret Jesuit headquarters for South Wales, but this was discovered by the authorities in Hereford and the house was raided in 1678.

In front of the churchyard cross at Welsh Newton is the grave of John Kemble, a Roman Catholic priest who was arrested at

Pembridge Castle, a mile north-west and, although over eighty, was executed at Hereford by the gruesome method of the time.

The simple inscription on his grave is:

I. K.
DYED THE 22 OF AUGUST
ANNO DOMINO
1679

A modern kerbstone has been added, stating that he was canonized in 1970. Next to it is another grave, found only in 1979, which may be that of either a Knight Templar or a Knight Hospitaller.

Until 1308, when the Order was dissolved in England, the church of St Mary the Virgin at Welsh Newton came under the jurisdiction of the Knights Templars' establishment at Garway. It then came into the hands of the Knights Hospitallers, whose principles were more acceptable to the Established Church. In their turn they lost their possessions during Henry VIII's Dissolution of the Monasteries.

Most of the church is thirteenth-century. Its heavy three-arched stone roodscreen lacks delicate tracery, but its ball flower decoration is an indication of its early fourteenth-century date. The rood gallery has gone, but the dormer window which once illuminated it can be seen in the side of the roof, while the only Romanesque feature is the Norman barrel-shaped font. On a wall inside the church are long hooks which are believed to have held fire-rakes for pulling burning thatch from the roof in case of fire, an ever-present risk when the church was thatched. Such rakes can be seen in many museums.

Pembridge Castle is easily missed as it lies back on the northeast side of the road, through a farm gate, and it is in fact part of the farm. From the gate a gravel drive leads down to the castle, which at the time of writing is open to the public on Thursdays. There is sufficient room to park a car adjoining the drawbridge and overlooking the moat, which still contains water. On the other side of the drawbridge is an imposing gatehouse, and you enter by a small inset door in the gatehouse into a courtyard, enclosed by the curtain wall of the castle. The castle was built mainly in the twelfth century, but to the left of the entrance is the seventeenth-century farmhouse, built against the curtain wall. The large round corner tower is probably the oldest part of the castle standing today and may be part of the original castle, said to have been built in 1135 by Ralph de Pembridge. The tower was probably the original keep, and on the east side a large arch apparently led to rooms which no longer exist. The imposing gatehouse is thirteenth century but was restored in the twentieth century. In the far corner of the courtyard is the sixteenth-century chapel, but the undercroft seems to be part of the original castle.

Like many castles, it received extensive damage during the Civil War and was in the hands of the Royalist garrison station at Monmouth but changed hands twice. It was subsequently repaired by George Kemble, who presumably built the present farmhouse and was of the same family as John Kemble, the martyred priest. The chapel and some parts of the castle were restored by Dr Hedley Bartlett, who bought the property in 1912. His cremated remains and those of his wife are buried in the chapel floor.

8

Monmouth to Ross

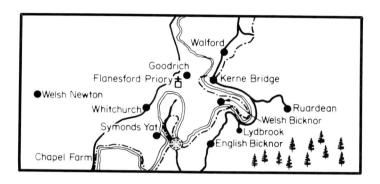

We leave the Monnow with its history of border strife and religious persecutions and plots and make our way down to the Wye. Above Monmouth the river makes a series of bends around forested hills and limestone escarpments, and in the narrowest and most precipitous part of the valley is Symonds Yat, the most popular part of the Wye Valley. The superb scenery of river and forest, the boat trips, the picnic and children's play areas, the several old inns and hotels attract visitors by car, in coaches and on foot during the summer months. The name Symonds Yat is believed to have been derived from that of a High Sheriff of Hereford in the seventeenth century, Robert Symonds, and the word 'yat', meaning a gate or a pass.

Overlooking the river on both sides is Yat Rock, where some parking places are provided, just a short walk from the finest viewpoint of this part of the river. Across the valley is the eyrie of the peregrine falcon, which started to nest here in 1981 after an absence of thirty years. In early spring I climbed the rough steps to the highest point and was lucky enough to meet the RSPB warden, who allowed me to look through his small telescope to see the female bird, a slender, buff-coloured shape against the dark ivy-covered cliff.

Yat Rock is the summit of a high peninsula around which the river makes a four-mile loop, and in the days of the Wye Tour the travellers from Ross would alight here, climb Yat Rock for the

Jubilee Maze, Whitchurch

exceptional view and descend the other side to board their boat again, which in the meantime had navigated the loop. The river then flows between Symonds Yat East and Symonds Yat West. These settlements are connected by two ferries, each operated by a boatman pulling a small flat boat across the river by means of an overhead cable.

In the boat, the *Wave*, built by Salter Brothers at Oxford in 1933, I lounge in the prow and watch the damsel flies, a smaller version of the dragonfly, with a glint of blue on their wings, flitting backwards and forwards in front of the boat. On one occasion the boatman, John Cronin, was telling his passengers that he had acquired the boat in 1935 and used to pick up passengers from the station. 'No station here now,' he said, pointing up to a stretch of typical railway fencing. 'That's all that's left of it, and the only transport on the track now is by foot!'

We had, at that point, just reached the top of the rapids. Several canoes were 'shooting' them, probably manned by a school group on an adventure holiday. Canoeing is the favourite sport, apart from fishing, on the Wye, particularly at this spot, where the rapids test the skill needed to negotiate the torrents and the rocks. It is quite usual to see mini-buses of young people with trailers carrying canoes, provided by one of the several centres in the forest, with expert wardens and tuition. Adjoining the rapids was once a large ironworks, powered by a waterwheel, the New Weir Forge, built in 1684. Surprisingly enough, it was one of the main attractions of the Wye Tour. The rapids were formed from the collapsed New Weir, and the adjoining lock, which enabled boats to navigate the river, has now gone, leaving an artificial island. Only a few stones of the old buildings remain, and the debris and iron ore washed into the river from the site have added to the turbulence of the rapids.

As John Cronin turned his craft away from the rapids, I noticed that there were shallows in the river, and it was not always possible to follow the boating rule of keeping to the right.

John told me, 'The last person to make the trip to Monmouth as a regular run was Trevor Williams, and rowing at that. The Williams family used to go to Monmouth with passengers but sometimes could only get as far as Chapel Farm, about 1½ miles short of Monmouth. Trevor Williams is still about, retired and settled at Goodrich.' As we turned into the landing stage, he called to two young people in a rowing-boat, 'Don't forget the time you came out.'

'You hire out rowing boats, too?' I asked.

'Oh, yes,' he said, 'and they're quite popular too.'

I added, 'There seems to be all varieties of craft on the river, rowing-boats, canoes, outboard engines.'

'Yes, barring battleships!' he replied. 'We small boatmen had all the trade here before they came,' and he cast a glance at one of the larger passenger boats.

On that occasion the river was more shallow than usual, owing to a long hot, dry spell. Cows were drinking in the water and, like a swan and some moorhens, were trying to get some shade from trees overhanging the bank. John Cronin told me that during a previous drought he saw forest deer in broad daylight, drinking at the water's edge, as most of the forest streams had dried up.

I left the *Wave* at its mooring adjoining the lower ferry near the Saracen's Head at Symonds Yat East and took the path on the east side of the river past the rapids for Biblins, passing a place called the Slaughter. This is a curious name and is popularly thought to refer to a particularly bloody battle, but legends vary about which battle. The stories range from Caractacus's last stand against the Romans, King Arthur's son's battle with the Danes, a battle with the Vikings and even a battle of the Civil War. However, there is an unromantic explanation, for the word 'slaughter' is thought to come from the Saxon *sloghtre*, meaning a muddy place, an apt description in wet weather. Better-known examples are probably the beautiful Cotswold villages of Upper and Lower Slaughter, collectively known as 'The Slaughters'.

At Biblins there is a remarkable suspension footbridge across the Wye, built by the Forestry Commission in 1957. Held by cables, it dips a lot in the middle, where I once stopped to look at a large salmon lying still in the clear water beneath me. The bridge shook as I walked on it, and on one occasion I had to stagger across with a large dog which refused to walk on the mesh floor which caught in its feet.

Across the bridge are some interesting rock formations, such as the Seven Sisters Rocks, and in the Lord's Wood high above them is King Arthur's Cave. The name is a mystery, for it appears to have no connection with the legendary king. It can be approached from the riverside by a steep path but is more easily reached from the top, where it is only a short distance by path from the road. The cave has a wide entrance but penetrates into the hill for only about fifteen yards. It must have been an ideal dwelling during the Stone Age, as a number of flint implements were found there in 1870–71 as well as bones of Ice Age animals. Some of the bones are in London's Natural History Museum, but a number of other finds are in Gloucester Museum.

In 1926 P. B. Symonds, a grandson of the original excavator, re-investigated the cave, assisted by the Bristol University Spelaeological Society, and many additional finds were made, including bones of mammoth, bison, hyaena, woolly rhinoceros, cave lion, cave bear and reindeer, animals extinct in the British Isles, with a further selection of flint implements. All periods were represented, from the palaeolithic to Roman times, and some of the items are in the Monmouth Museum but many were destroyed when the Society's museum was bombed during the last war in an air attack on Bristol.

At the same time the Bristol University Spelaeological Society dug in another cave, which they called Merlin's Cave, in a steep slope about 150 feet above the Wye, near Old Forge. This was a passage about six to ten feet wide in places and running into the hill for about fifty feet. There was not the vast amount of material which was found in King Arthur's Cave, but the cave produced items belonging to the same range of time. Both King Arthur's Cave and Merlin's Cave had once been dug into by miners looking for iron or other minerals. These miners were also responsible for the shallow pits seen in the neighbouring woods.

Although wall pictures of mammoth, bison and other pleistocene animals have been found, particularly in France and Spain, no cave wall art has ever been discovered in Britain, but a few years ago Canadian-born Dr Tom Rogers, when exploring a cave with two companions in the area of Symonds Yat, believed he had discovered the mutilated engraving of a bison on the wall of the cave and another of the head of a deer-like animal on a rock face some fifty yards from the cave. Considerable publicity was given to these discoveries and, if genuine, they would have been of immense importance as the first examples of palaeolithic cave wall art to be found in Britain. However, the principal British experts in the subject examined the markings, and their opinion was that they were made by the natural weathering of the rock and not by man.

Across the river from King Arthur's Cave and the Seven Sisters Rocks is the Far Hearkening Rock with Near Hearkening Rock over half a mile south in High Meadow Woods. These rocks were said to have peculiar acoustic properties, and gamekeepers used to wait here listening for poachers. Just before Near Hearkening

Rock is the Suckstone, some sixty feet long, said to be the largest boulder in Britain. Some people think it was a ley-line marker on a pagan communication route, and, in fact, a line taken from King Arthur's Cave and Seven Sisters Rocks through the Suckstone and the Hearkening Rocks meets another huge boulder, the Buckstone, on a ridge near Staunton.

The Buckstone was a logan or rocking stone and is the subject of several legends. One says that it was a druid's altar stone and, if walked round three times, would fulfil a wish. Another legend says it was used by the Britons as a look-out, and sentries would rock the stone on the approach of enemies, so that the sound of the rocking could be heard by the tribes living in the valley below. Whatever the truth in these stories, the Buckstone has not rocked since 1885, when a party of unruly visitors decided to rock it off its perch. Subsequently this massive block of Old Red Sandstone conglomerate was once again set up on the ridge, but as a fixture to prevent this happening again. It is one of the many natural logans known throughout the world.

By the river at Symonds Yat West is the Garden Leisure Centre, adjoining a landing-stage where boatmen offer river trips. Next to the entrance of the Centre is the lane to the ancient church of St Dubricius, the Whitchurch parish church which serves Symonds Yat. The church stands close to the bank and is one of the sights pointed out by the river boatmen. It was often flooded, particularly in 1947 and 1960, but it is hoped that the problem has been solved by recent riverworks. The site is apt for such a dedication, for St Dubricius was a Welsh saint, whose Welsh name was Dyfrig, meaning a water child. According to legend, Dyfrig's mother was the daughter of a Welsh king, who was angry at her unexplained pregnancy and, determined to wipe out the disgrace by her death, had her tied up in a sack and thrown into the water, presumably the Wye. She escaped from the sack and was washed ashore. Her father then demanded that she be burnt to death, but the fire did not harm her and the next day she gave birth to Dubricius. Whatever the real story of his birth, he grew up to found many churches and became a bishop. Eventually he lived as a hermit on Bardsey Island until he died about AD 546.

'Whitchurch' is a typically English place-name, probably derived from 'white church', for we are now in Herefordshire, but only just. St Dubricius's church is mostly fourteenth-century with traces of thirteenth-century work, although the circular font is Norman. The churchyard cross is fifteenth-century, but with a

Church of St Dubricius, Whitchurch

modern cross head. Near the cross is an enormous tulip tree, a
native forest tree of America, where it can grow to a height of
about 200 feet. In Britain it is planted as an ornamental tree and
rarely exceeds eighty feet. It was a custom of early American
settlers to send young tulip trees to relatives and friends in Britain
and elsewhere. It is akin to the magnolia, and its tulip-like flowers
are yellowish green on the outside and orange inside. In America
it is felled to produce tulipwood for furniture.

Adjoining the lane to the church, wrought-iron gates lead to a
maze – a word akin to 'amazing', and the Jubilee Maze is
certainly that. It is open to the public, and for six evenings weekly
in the high summer it is illuminated after dark.

On my first visit to the maze, I was met by the brothers Lindsay
and Edward Heyes, who were responsible for its creation. They
were both wearing blazers and boaters, giving a nice Edwardian
touch to the scene. They had planted the maze in 1977 to
celebrate the Queen's Silver Jubilee, and it was first open to the

public on the day of the Royal Wedding of Prince Charles and Lady Diana, in 1981. I asked them why they had created a maze and was told that their parents owned the adjoining Whitchurch House, the old rectory, reputed to have been the home of one of the victims of the 'Brides in the Bath' murder case and now used as a home for the elderly. When the adjacent orchard came on the market, their parents bought it to prevent noisy or unsightly development and present it to their two sons to put to some unobjectionable use, provided no structures were erected to obscure the view from the house. They decided to build a maze which they set out to their own design, planting four-foot-high evergreens, now kept to a convenient height and beautifully trimmed. There is a small museum with photographs and drawings of the history and legends of mazes from all over the world.

It was suggested that my small party should split and start off in the maze in opposite directions to see who would reach the centre first. After various wrong turnings and culs-de-sac, we arrived at the centre and found there the 'Temple of Diana'. There is no risk of being lost in the maze, as immediately outside is a viewing platform from which directions can be given if necessary. Near the exit is the 'Royal Bed', so called

Jubilee Maze, Whitchurch

because all the flowers and shrubs have some association with royalty.

It was sheltered in the maze, but when I came out a cold wind was blowing and it was pleasant to escape to the 'World of Butterflies', in an enormous glasshouse owned by Barrie Jones. Here, flitting among the exotic shrubs and plants, brilliant with flowers, were large tropical butterflies, some as colourful as the flowers themselves. At one side were creatures enclosed in wall cages, stick insects, scorpions, tarantulas and even tropical spiders. Barrie Jones told me that at times there are about 700 butterflies, sometimes more, although he likes to keep them to about that number. Most of his butterflies live for only about sixteen days, although one or two species live rather longer. At first the chrysalides were imported from abroad, but now he breeds them locally. Indeed he has some hatching chrysalides on display. By careful planning, a constant supply of the various types is produced to maintain the fine show. You can buy posters, pictures, books and mounted specimens in the adjoining shop.

Between 1985 and 1986 considerable tourist development has taken place at this end of Symonds Yat West, around the Jubilee Maze, with the World of Butterflies, the Symonds Yat Bird Park, a large parking area, a tea-room and a proposal for a craft workshop.

Further along the Wye and to the east of Symonds Yat is English Bicknor. St Mary's Church stands within the edge of a motte-and-bailey, on which a Norman castle once stood, guarding the Wye crossing, but the only remaining traces are pieces of Norman work found in the motte. The outside of the church is thirteenth- to fifteenth-century and it is surprising to find Norman work inside. On the north side of the nave, adjoining the thirteenth-century chancel, is a fine Norman arch, embellished with typical Norman chevrons and seven animal heads supported on colonnettes. The arches of the nave arcade are carried on short Norman columns.

A decorated tomb chest stands in the churchyard to the left of the church doorway. The inscription is worn but still legible and reads: 'And also Anne the wife of John Liblamb, Gent. daughter of John Jordan by Elizabeth his wife was born March 16th 1695 and buried October 25th 1708.' The bride was only thirteen years and seven months old when she died and is an example of child marriage of that time. Her epitaph has these rather charming lines:

St Margaret's church, Welsh Bicknor

> If I could ever write a Latin verse
> It should be laid dear saint upon your hearse
> A beauteous blossom so untimely dead
> Whither oh whither is thy sweetness fled
> Where are those charms that did adorn thy mind
> So humble, meek, so easy and so kind.

From English Bicknor there is a beautiful ride down to the Wye, but spoilt at one corner by a chimney and a collection of factory buildings adjoining the road – fortunately they are left behind as quickly as they appear. Further along the river, Welsh Bicknor church can be seen on the opposite bank. Welsh Bicknor, like Welsh Newton, is not now in Wales, although the river and Offa's Dyke, which passes between English and Welsh Bicknor, were once the boundaries between England and Wales. Just

Goodrich Castle

beyond the church, a large white house, with modern extensions, comes into view, high up near the top of the slope. It was at Courtfield that the future Henry V, the prince born at Monmouth Castle, is said to have been nursed by the Countess of Salisbury. It is doubtful whether an effigy in Welsh Bicknor church is that of the Countess, as Henry was born in the late fourteenth century, while the dress style of the effigy is that of a century earlier. During the nineteenth century, Courtfield was the home of the Vaughan family, including Cardinal Vaughan, whose mother belonged to the Rolls family. He did much to help establish the Roman Catholic Cathedral at Westminster and was keen on the provision of training colleges for young priests. It is fitting today that Courtfield is a Catholic seminary under the control of the Mill Hill fathers.

The Anglican church of St Margaret on the river bank is a Victorian restoration, occupying quite an isolated position and usually kept locked. The equally isolated building nearby was once the rectory but is now a youth hostel. The church can be approached by the Wye Valley Walk along the banks of the river or from Goodrich by road up Coppet Hill, where there are some fine views through the trees of Kerne Bridge and the Wye. Finally, you arrive at the gates to Courtfield and at the right a lane leads to the youth hostel. Part way down this lane a footpath directs you to the church, but it is steep and can be muddy and dangerous.

To the east of Welsh Bicknor and the river is Ruardean in the Forest of Dean. Its area was once a bailiwick – that is, a section of the Forest under the jurisdiction of a forester of fee, who was responsible to the constable at St Briavels Castle. Under him were other foresters to assist him in his duties in protecting the forest and the venison, a term which today means deer meat but which under the old forest laws included the wild deer and boar which roamed the forest. The forester of fee enjoyed certain privileges which could include wood-gathering and falconry. Wyrall, whose fascinating tomb is in Newland church, was a forester of fee.

St John the Baptist Church at Ruardean has an outstanding feature, a tympanum, probably of about 1150, carved with St George and the Dragon, over the inner doorway. The tower and spire were built in the fourteenth century, and the inevitable restoration work was carried out in 1890. Ruardean is located on some of the highest ground in the forest, and the top of the spire is 1,000 feet above sea-level. Round the churchyard is one of the finest collections of carved tombstones in the forest, and in the churchyard are tombs of the Horlick family. James Horlick was the founder of the milk-drink company and was born in Ruardean, but it was not until the family moved from Ruardean that he invented the drink.

Years ago, to mention bears in Ruardean was like the proverbial red rag to a bull. 'Who killed the bears?' was a taunt once used by foresters outside Ruardean. The story originated from the time when performing bears were taken round the countryside, and once rumour was put round Ruardean that one of these bears had killed a child. Irate men set out and, according to Harry Beddington, who tells the story in a fascinating dialect poem 'Who Killed the Bears?', they were armed 'wi' sticks an' stwuns an' iron bars, brick-bats an' chuncks of 'ood' and they killed the bears. As the rumour turned out to be unfounded, the men of Ruardean at that time were the butt of taunts from their neighbours. I can't imagine that the remark would provoke any reaction today, as the story is probably forgotten, but perhaps it would be as well, if you are in Ruardean, not to ask 'Who killed the bears?'.

After making the circuit of Coppet Hill, the peninsula, with Welsh Bicknor church and Courtfield, the Wye can be followed to Goodrich, with its imposing shell of a castle. Masked to some extent by the village, it is perhaps best seen from the wooded slopes on the other bank, although the views of the countryside from the castle are magnificent. The oldest part of the castle is its grey stone Norman keep, originally entered by an external staircase to the first floor, a not-unusual arrangement making the occupants less vulnerable to attack. The ground floor acted as a store and sometimes as a dungeon. The keep is only twenty-nine feet square with limited living-space, and so more commodious quarters were built in sandstone in the thirteenth century, consisting principally of a great hall, sixty-five feet long with kitchens nearby, a change from the original main room on the upper floor of the keep. The old quarters could still serve as a useful haven in the event of an attack.

The castle was, in fact, attacked by the Parliamentarian army in 1646. It was so strongly built on a well-defended site that it was one of the last Royalist-held castles to fall to Parliament. It was held for the Royalists by Sir Henry Lingen but he survived to become a Member of Parliament for Hereford. Colonel Birch, who besieged the castle for four months before its surrender, had a niece, Alice, who was in love with Charles Clifford, a Royalist

Goodrich Castle Interior

St Giles's church, Goodrich

helping to defend the castle. Somehow she managed to join him, and together they escaped through the besieging force, but the Wye was in flood and they were drowned crossing the river. Legend has it that their cries can still be heard above the roar of the water, and Andrew Green in his book *Our Haunted Kingdom* refers to a story that on stormy nights the ghosts of a rider with a lady behind him have been seen trying to force their horse into the torrent. Colonel Birch eventually took the castle by using a great mortar known as 'Roaring Meg'.

Goodrich church, St Giles, is not easy to find. The thirteenth-century church is approached by a lane and then a footpath, just south and above the village on the hillside in an isolated position. At the time of the Civil War, Thomas Swift, the grandfather of Dean Swift, was the vicar. He was a staunch Royalist, a great supporter of Sir Henry Lingen, and devised methods of delaying the Parliamentarian advance. He was so loyal that he mortgaged his estate and sewed the proceeds into a quilted waistcoat to avoid seizure by his opponents, taking the gold to the King, who was staying at Raglan Castle after the Battle of Naseby. As a Royalist

Flanesford Priory

supporter, Parliament deprived him of his living as vicar of Goodrich.

From Goodrich Castle can be seen what is left of Flanesford Priory, an Augustinian establishment built in 1346. Practically all that is left of the priory is its refectory, incorporated in a farm-house adjoining Kerne Bridge and easily viewed from the road. It was only a small establishment, but what there is remains in very good condition.

A combined visit to Flanesford and Goodrich Castle was one of the stops on the Wye Tour. There was no Kerne Bridge before 1828, and the boats of the Wye Tour would moor on the opposite bank to allow their occupants to take the ferry to cross the river, maybe because the opposite bank was easier for disembarking or because of restrictions on mooring on the Flanesford Priory bank. On the other hand, was it collusion between the Wye Tour operators and the ferryman?

It is said that when, in 1387, the future Henry IV came to take the ferry on his way to Monmouth, he was met by the ferryman with the news that his son, the future Henry V, had been born in

Monmouth Castle. On hearing the news, the delighted father granted the ferryman the ownership of the ferry and the life-long right to carry people across the Wye.

About a mile north of Kerne Bridge and near the east bank of the Wye is Walford, obviously one of the original fords across the river – but why the 'Wal'? It is possible that it may be derived from 'Wales' or 'Welsh'. There was some kind of settlement here during the latter part of the Roman occupation, for no fewer than 18,000 Roman coins in three urns were found at Walford during the last century. Without banks, the safest way to keep money was to bury it in the ground, provided you remembered where you buried it. The presence of such a hoard indicates that there was at least one farmstead, Roman villa or settlement at Walford.

The thirteenth-century church of St Michael had its spire struck by lightning in 1813, and the old top is in the churchyard. Over the chancel arch hangs a helm, and a story goes that it belonged to Colonel Birch, who is believed to have stayed at a farmhouse in Walford, while conducting the siege of Goodrich Castle. This, however, is hardly likely, as the helm is a funerary helm, an armoured helmet carried at a knight's funeral as an indication of rank. Other armour equipment was often included in the funeral regalia, such as spurs, and it is not unusual to find such items hung in churches. The helmet at Walford dates to 1600 and would have been old-fashioned by the time Colonel Birch was in the neighbourhood. There seems to be no reason why he should have left his helmet behind.

The road outside the church is reputedly haunted by the ghost of a headless monk, and on the opposite side of the road a public footpath leads up the hill, thick with bluebells in spring. At one point there is a splendid view of Goodrich Castle, particularly fine in the morning, when the sun is on the warm red sandstone walls. Along this path is a white cottage, once the home of Robert Pashley, a renowned fisherman of the 1930s who had a favourite place on the Wye known as Dog Hole. In one year, Pashley caught no fewer than forty tons of salmon, enough to fill a trawler. In those days the Wye was so full of salmon that it was almost possible to cross the river by stepping on them, surely an exaggeration, but now the number of salmon has been much depleted. In the village there is a memorial hall to Robert Pashley. He lived during the 1930's and when he died, he left £2,000 to a local school, and the pupils still benefit from the interest.

9

In and Around Ross

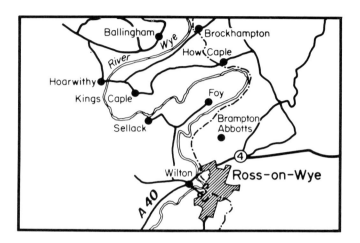

Ross-on-Wye is a town of some character, with one of those ancient market houses at its centre, close to an interesting church, old streets and almshouses and with a pleasant river front. The approach across the Wilton Bridge presents an imposing view of the town, standing high above the river on red sandstone cliffs, capped with mock-medieval walls, like some ancient fortified settlement. Above the walls appear the 205-foot church spire, a landmark for miles around, and the white buildings of the Royal Hotel. It has been suggested that the red colour of the rock has given the town its name, derived from the Welsh word *rhos*, meaning roses, but it is more likely to have come from another meaning of *rhos*: a peninsula or heath.

The red sandstone church of St Mary the Virgin was begun in 1284, a spacious building, much restored. Your attention is drawn almost immediately to the mass of funeral monuments on a dais in the south aisle to the right of the chancel. It seems as if all the tomb effigies in the church had been piled into one corner with hardly room to move between them. They are of the Rudhall family, and towering above the rest stands the effigy of Colonel William Rudhall, depicted in Roman armour, hand on sword.

The Market House, Ross

Dressed to kill, he seems in an inappropriate setting and would look better in a park or on the top of a column. It is true that, like Horatio, he defended a bridge, but that was Wilton Bridge during the Civil War, and the Colonel would hardly have appeared at the head of his Royalist troops in the costume of a Roman centurion – a costume of the Stuart period might have been expected to match his Cavalier pointed beard and locks. There he stands like the survivor of a massacre surrounded by recumbent bodies.

The other effigies in the group are more informative about the costume and appearance of their time, and about their children who are depicted on the sides of the tombs. Those who pre-deceased their parents are shown with skulls, and on one tomb chest is carved a baby in swaddling clothes propped on a skull.

On the wall of the sanctuary is a monument to John Kyrle, born 1637. One cannot write or talk about Ross without referring to John Kyrle, 'the Man of Ross'. He came to Ross about 1660, ten years after the death of Colonel Rudhall, and became a great benefactor to the town. He improved and restored the church, gave the town a water supply and a public park, rebuilt the old causeway over the marshland to Wilton Bridge and helped the poor with his generous gifts. His title of 'the Man of Ross' was bestowed upon him by Alexander Pope in his *Third Moral Epistle*, published in 1732. It was praise indeed from a poet who usually wrote scathing lines about his contemporaries and so gained his own title of 'the Wicked Asp of Twickenham'. Pope admired Kyrle and lamented the fact that no memorial had been erected to him, an omission rectified when the church tablet was set up in 1776, and in the early twentieth century a further memorial to the great benefactor was a clock added to the church tower. His grave is under the carpet in the chancel. The town itself does not let you forget him. It has a public house called 'The Man of Ross', and his name appears over the house where he once lived behind the Market House and where he died in 1724. After Kyrle's time, this fine timber-framed 'black-and-white' house was used as an inn, and Coleridge once stayed there.

The Market House, of red sandstone, set up on columns to allow space for the market on ground level, is the most conspicuous building in Ross. On the outside of the east wall is a bust of Charles II, which replaced the original badly eroded bust. John Kyrle was a firm supporter of the monarchy and is said to have been disappointed that he could not see the figure of the King from his house, so, at his request, a plaque with the entwined

John Kyrle's House, Ross

letters F.C. enclosed in a heart, said to mean 'Faithful to Charles in Heart', was put up on the wall of the Market House facing his windows.

A walk of 2½ miles round Ross was a favourite stroll of Kyrle's and is known today as 'John Kyrle's Walk'. At the far side of the churchyard is the Prospect, a small public park which he gave to the town. It is enclosed within high walls, with two stone gateways, and the far side commands wonderful views of the Wye and the surrounding countryside. In one corner is a cross commemorating those who died in the two Great Wars and one victim of the Falkland campaign of recent times.

Ross owes so much to John Kyrle that it is a wonder that its name was never changed to Kyrle's Town but, as can be expected, there is a Kyrle Street and a John Kyrle School. The

original Kyrle Society was formed in 1877 to encourage the laying-out of parks and gardens and the maintenance of houses to keep Ross the pleasant place that Kyrle would have wished it to be.

Near the church, a square memorial surmounted by an urn covers the grave of Walter Scott, not the novelist but another benefactor of the town who died in 1786. He was a local carpenter's son who, in the best Dick Whittington tradition, went to London and made his fortune. He left £7,000 to rebuild the Blue Coat School. Unfortunately in 1928 the school closed through lack of funds, but some money is still used to assist deserving young parishioners with their education.

A tragic memorial is the Plague Cross in the corner of the churchyard by the steps leading down to Church Street. This old cross bears a small weather-worn plaque to the memory of 315 victims of plague in 1637 and who are buried in the open area of the churchyard just to the west of the cross.

Opposite the steps into Church Street are the double-storeyed Rudhall Almshouses, rebuilt in 1575. They are of the local red sandstone and consist of five dwellings, each having its own gable and attic window. The occupants in John Kyrle's time enjoyed the food which he sent to them every day.

Among the modern buildings in Ross is the Phoenix Theatre Arts Centre, an attractive little building in a cul-de-sac jammed between the Royal Hotel and the churchyard, which is at its roof level. The Royal Hotel had many distinguished visitors in the nineteenth century, including Queen Victoria and Princess Mary of Teck, later to become Queen Mary. Here, in 1867, Charles Dickens met his friend John Forster, the son of a cattle-dealer who wrote several biographies – but his *Life of Charles Dickens* is thought to be the best.

Opposite the hotel, a tower and so-called town walls appear ancient at first sight but date only from the 1830s, when the new approach road was made up from the riverside. This involved cutting into the cliffs, and the 'ancient' walls provided a bit of landscaping. Steep Wye Street, with eighteenth- and nineteenth-century houses, leads down to the river, which, with its riverside Rope Walk, is a great feature of Ross. Here we find the Hope and Anchor Inn, once popular with the boatmen and passengers of the river traffic from Hereford to Chepstow and now equally popular among visitors for its river views, bars and restaurants. It was once a basket-making centre.

Ross from inside the Market Hall

Rudhall almshouses

On the other side of the river is Wilton, connected with Ross by Wilton Bridge, built in 1597–9. In the middle recess of the bridge is a tall, early eighteenth-century sundial, with the inscription:

Esteem thy precious time
Which pass so swift away
Prepare thee for eternity
And do not make delay.

You do well to take heed of these lines as you approach the sundial, as the pavement is very narrow on that side of the bridge, only wide enough for one person and the traffic fast and heavy. The other side of the bridge has lost its recesses because of road-widening. During the plague of 1637 commemorated by the cross in Ross churchyard, it is believed that the recesses were used for leaving goods, so that the traders would not have to enter the stricken town. Traditionally coins for payment were left in bowls of vinegar, an early disinfectant.

From the bridge can be seen the ruins of Wilton Castle among the trees to the north. It is in private grounds, not open to the public. During the Civil War it was held by the Royalists and subsequently destroyed. Before the present Wilton Bridge there was a wooden bridge across the Wye, and before that a ford. The castle was erected in the thirteenth century to protect the ford and so was built close to the river. In the time of Henry I, the castle was held by Hugh de Longchamp, who furnished the King with two soldiers for war against the Welsh. The Grey family occupied it from the latter part of the thirteenth century and held it until Queen Mary's reign, when William, Lord Grey, fought in defence of Calais. It then passed to the first Lord Chandos, who married Lord Grey's sister. Later the castle was acquired by Thomas Guy, who gave it to the hospital he founded in London.

Close to the northern boundary of Ross is Brampton Abbotts, whose church of St Michael and All Angels was founded about 1100. Some Norman work remains, such as the south doorway, but the church was much restored in 1857 and again in 1907–8. The large stone in the chancel was once the cover stone of the Rudhall vault and commemorates John Rudhall and his wife, Joan.

A little more than a mile north of Brampton Abbotts is Foy, situated on a peninsula around which the river makes a circuit of several miles. It can be reached from the south by an attractive foot suspension bridge, built in the 1930s, replacing one of 1876. Yat Rock at Symonds Yat stands on such a peninsula, but at Foy

The Hope and Anchor, Ross

Wilton Bridge, Ross

the river banks border on lush meadows in contrast to the woodlands and rocky banks at Symonds Yat.

St Mary's Church at Foy dates from the early fourteenth century, although both Decorated and Perpendicular work feature. The east window is a copy of an original window in Sellack church, through a bequest in the seventeenth century by John Abrahall, for such a window to be provided in Foy church.

From the south-east end of the suspension bridge, there is a pleasant riverside drive to How Caple. This is one of the few stretches where you can drive with a long uninterrupted view of the Wye, often with no more than one field sloping down to the water, between the road and the river and with woods rising above the road on the other side.

The church at How Caple is not easy to find. A very small direction board on the road leading from Crossway points down a lane, and some way down, a wide doorway leads into the courtyard behind How Caple Court, with a shop in one of the outbuildings, selling fabrics, bags of fuel, firewood and special horsefood. A key of the church is kept here and also at the post office near the entrance to the lane. Beyond the courtyard, the unsurfaced lane dips steeply to the church of St Andrew and St Mary. Although of Norman origin, the church was rebuilt in 1695, and the most ancient structural part remaining is the thirteenth- to fourteenth-century chancel. The chancel screen was apparently added in 1695, and its design is unusual. It has a balustrade with twisted balusters and twisted columns. Above are the arms of William III. There are two pulpits, one on either side of the screen, but the one on the right is the more interesting. It is Jacobean with a sounding-board or tester, copied from that in Oxford Cathedral.

The late Norman octagonal font was found in the garden of How Caple Court and was reinstated in the church, while the 1698 font was placed in the churchyard in front of the blocked south door. The 1695 rebuilding was carried out by Sir William Gregory, who had just bought the estate from the Capels who had lived in the Court since the twelfth century. The present owners, the Lee family, acquired it in 1901 and made improvements to the church. They added the Parliament clock which hangs on the wall.

How Caple is associated with a miracle concerning a boy who fell from his father's moored boat in 1300 and was apparently drowned. The boy, Nicholas Fisher, was seen to fall into the river by Margaret Francis from the opposite bank. Later his body was recovered and placed in a warm bed. There seemed no doubt that he was dead, but it was agreed to offer a candle to St Thomas de Cantilupe of Hereford. A few hours later the boy recovered and in the following week the family and a large body of villagers went to Hereford Cathedral to report the miracle. St Thomas had been considered a saint by local people for some years but was not canonized until after the drowning incident – in fact, not until 1320. This was one of the miracles accepted by the papal commissioners who came to the district in 1307 to consider the canonization, because of the large number of miracles reported in connection with St Thomas, who was buried in Hereford Cathedral. Of the 200 examined, seventeen were accepted as genuine miracles, including the How Caple incident.

St Tysilio's Church at Sellack contains bits and pieces of architecture, Norman, Early English and Victorian, and the east window is a mixture of fifteenth-, sixteenth- and seventeenth-century glass. The pulpit is Jacobean.

To the north of Sellack is King's Caple and St John the Baptist's Church is one of the churches in the district where Pax

Cakes are distributed to the congregation on Palm Sunday (as does St Tysilio's, Sellack). When a Scudamore, a member of the great local family, whose ancestral home was Holme Lacy House, made a bequest to provide funds for the ceremony, it was called 'Cake Money'.

The church tower is fourteenth century, with ball-flower decoration of that period on a string course. Inside the church is a Jacobean pulpit with its soundingboard, panelled stalls and two box pews. It would have been difficult to doze unnoticed within the walls of the box pews of the period during a tedious sermon as the preacher, from his lofty perch, had quite a good view of his congregation. Most of the box pews, which were once common, have been swept away in favour of bench pews, but quite a number of the tall Jacobean pulpits remain. Some have lost their soundingboards, or testers, and others have had their two or three tiers reduced to one. However, they are usually quite easily recognized by the typical wooden panelling, often distinguished by a border at the top of a continuous run of semi-circular arches, a decoration common on carved domestic furniture of the time. At the beginning of the seventeenth century there seems to have been a spate of installing wooden Jacobean pulpits, among the most attractive of church furnishings. In St John's Church there are two fine nineteenth-century memorials, both by leading sculptors of their day, one to Mrs Holcombe Ferguson, teaching her young son, by John Flaxman, and the other to Eliza Woodhouse, shown as a mourning woman with an urn, by Richard Westmacott.

Crossing the bridge, we come to Hoarwithy, an Anglo-Saxon name for the whitebeam. The Italianate-Byzantine church of St Catherine looks oddly out of place in the Wye Valley; it would be at home in an Italian mountain village and, although it stands high on the hill overlooking Hoarwithy, it lacks the appropriate countryside. It was designed by J. P. Seddon in 1885 to meet the whim of the vicar, William Poole. The church is reached from the road by a steep, straight path, incorporating flights of steps, an impressive approach which leads the eye upwards to an archway piercing the base of a very tall *campanile*, carrying the eye even further upwards to the pierced bell openings, through which glimpses of daylight can be seen. As we approach the arch, the huge apse end of the building rises above on the right, the typical east apse end of Romanesque church architecture of southern France. Passing through the arch, we enter a long gallery running along the side of the church, its double columns and elaborately carved capitals like many European Romanesque cloister walks. Turning at the end of the gallery, we come to the entrance door at the west end and, entering, find ourselves in what appears to be a complete Byzantine interior, high and light, embellished with marble and mosaic. No expense was spared in construction or in decoration. It is a mixture of styles borrowed from France and Italy, with much of the interior design from Puy in France and San Vitale at Ravenna, Italy. The design of the hanging lamps has been borrowed from the pendants of St Mark's, Venice, that of the pulpit from Fiesole Cathedral, above Florence, and it even had a hypocaust, underfloor heating used in Roman baths.

The cost of the building was met by Poole from his own rentals from the properties he had inherited, and it replaced a chapel which he described as an 'ugly building with no pretensions to any style of architecture'. Some of the brickwork of the original chapel is incorporated into the present building. St Catherine's certainly has pretensions, but to several styles of architecture, Romanesque, Italian and Byzantine, and it lacks the atmosphere and 'soul' of the ancient buildings from which it derives its inspiration. However, it is a refreshing surprise to find such a building in a Herefordshire village and an interesting change from the usual Victorian Gothic, often spelt 'Gothick' to distinguish the pseudo from the original medieval style. A good view of St Catherine's can be seen from the car-park of the New Harp public house opposite the old mill. From this viewpoint the complete side of the church with its cloister-type gallery can be seen on the top of the hill.

About a mile north-west of How Caple is Brockhampton, where there is yet another unusual church, much smaller than that at Hoarwithy and of a more original design. It must have made quite a stir in its day, following hard on Victorian Gothic, being not of mixed architectural styles, as at Hoarwithy, but of a strange contrast of materials: concrete, stone and thatch. Many small country churches had originally thatched roofs, but not in 1901–2, when this church was built. The church of All Saints was designed by W. R. Lethaby, an ardent follower of the William Morris School and the Arts and Crafts Movement, and here there is a feeling of simple country crafts and values. The steeply arched walls and ceiling are reminiscent of the ancient cruck structure, when split, rough, curved timbers were used as the main supports. Although certain structural principles were followed, Lethaby introduced a style using completely different material.

All Saints church, Brockhampton

The roof is concrete but clad with thatch, the traditional roofing material which blends in with its country background.

Everywhere inside the church are designs based on the flowers and foliage of the countryside. The font designed by Lethaby is decorated with vines. There are flowers carved on the wooden panelling, and the altar frontal cloth is embroidered with floral designs. There are local wild flowers beautifully embroidered on the linen hymn-book covers which were found one day left on the altar by an anonymous donor. On either side of the altar are magnificent tapestries depicting angels. These were from the William Morris workshops from a design by Burne-Jones.

Lethaby was not the only architect to break with the traditions of the time, but he was one of the most outstanding. This new architecture was only part of a wider movement in the arts and philosophy, a movement away from the artificiality and ugliness of the Machine Age. It was largely inspired by William Morris, whose workshops produced fabrics, coloured glass and other material with designs based on natural forms. As a young man, Lethaby spent twelve years in the office of Norman Shaw, himself a rebel, who designed New Scotland Yard, and under him Lethaby seems to have developed his own particular style. He was

All Saints church, Brockhampton

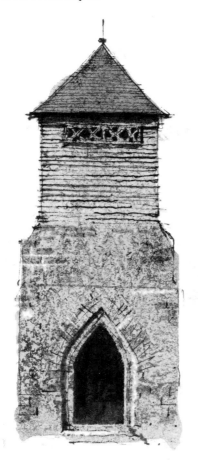

The old church, Brockhampton

Brockhampton Court Lodge

forty-four when he created Brockhampton church, and there is little doubt that this was the beginning of the major part of his career. At that time he was Professor of Design at the Royal College of Art, and from 1908 to 1921 he published several books on architectural themes, ranging from Greek to modern architecture.

The churchyard at Brockhampton is as pleasing as the church and gained recognition as the best-kept churchyard by winning the S. A. Evans Trophy. A solid tablet set up in a conspicuous place in the corner of the churchyard records this award – so solid a notice that perhaps it is to ensure that the surroundings will always be kept in the same condition.

Opposite the church are the drive to Brockhampton Court and the ruins of the old Holy Trinity Church. The Court itself was once a hospital and is now an hotel. The original part of the building was the rectory in the eighteenth century. At the entrance to the drive is the lodge, an eye-catching pseudo black-and-white building, used as a post office.

The full name of Brockhampton is Brockhampton by Ross, not to be confused with Brockhampton by Bromyard, further to the north.

Across the Wye is Ballingham, where the church, like those at Whitchurch and Hentland, is dedicated to St Dubricius. Pevsner describes it as being 'over-restored' – the work done in 1884–5. However, the tower is probably late thirteenth-century, as is one small lancet window in the fourteenth-century nave. We find here a memorial tablet to a William Scudamore who died in 1649.

Although the name of the village is English enough, the dedication of the church is to an early saint who became the first Bishop of Llandaff. St Dubricius was associated with an area of Herefordshire known as Archenfield, whose eastern edge included Ballingham. This was the Welsh kingdom of Erging, between the Monnow and the Wye, including much of the south-western corner of the English county. It formed a kind of buffer state between England and the turbulent Welsh of the border country. The Normans recognized the advantage of this arrangement and allowed Archenfield (or Erging) to continue as an independent state, keeping its customs and language and enjoying privileges in return for services to the Normans. Even in the eighteenth century there were people in this little Wales in England who could speak nothing but Welsh. Today it is very much part of the county of Hereford & Worcester, but there are still traces of the old kingdom in some place-names and dedications of churches. St Dubricius is one.

10

Towards Hereford

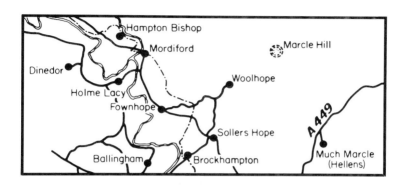

Sollers Hope, to the north-east of Brockhampton, is to be found on the east side of the Wye – that is, if you can find it, with the old church at the end of a track, next to a splendid timber-framed house with a couple of fine chimneystacks, making an attractive grouping.

'Hope' is common in place-names in this part of the Wye Valley and is usually taken to mean a hollow in the side of a hill. It is one of the places where Dick Whittington is said to have been born, although at least one other place, Pauntley, in Gloucestershire, makes a similar claim, as Pauntley Court was the home of the Whittington family up to 1543. According to Dugdale, Whittington claimed that his father's name was William and his mother's Joan. Sir William Whittington lived at Pauntley and married Joan Mansel, so Pauntley would appear to have the stronger claim than Sollers Hope. However, as the places are in adjoining counties, it seems certain that he came from that part of the country. We do know that Richard Whittington did exist, that he became Mayor of London three times, amassed a great fortune and died in March 1423. He was not knighted and whether he won his fortune when his cat rid the palace of a foreign potentate of the rats and mice which infested it is a matter of doubt.

The first reference to the cat seems to have been in a lost play of 1605. Similar cat stories have been found in Italy, Persia and Denmark, dating back as far as the thirteenth century. The usual

Mordiford Bridge

version of this story is that, as a destitute orphan, the only
contribution he had to make to his master's seafaring venture was
his cat, and the clever animal won him a fortune. Or he might
have owned a catt, a shallow-bottomed vessel used in the Port
of London. Was this the catt he sent on his master's venture to
make his fortune? Cat or catt, if he was the son of Sir William
Whittington, he certainly did not start life as a destitute orphan.

The fourteenth- to fifteenth-century church of St Michael, at
Sollers Hope, commemorates its connection with the Whittington
family in the modern tiles in front of the altar. These are decorated
with various coats of arms, including those of the Whittingtons,
and a description displayed in the church mentions that much of
the finance for its early restoration was provided by Robert, a
brother of Dick Whittington. On the south side of the chancel is
an early thirteenth-century coffin slab with the incised figure of an
armoured knight bearing the arms of the Solas family, discovered
when the vestry was being built in 1887, with three other coffin
lids.

On the same parallel as Sollers Hope and further to the east is
Much Marcle, where we find Hellens, an interesting old mansion
in private ownership but open to the public on Saturday, Sunday
and Wednesday afternoons in the summer. The name is derived
from a family name, Helyon – but whose family? The usual story
is that Walter Helyon was a steward who managed the estate in
the fourteenth century and lived in the house during the absence
of the owners, so that it became known locally as Helyon's house
or Hellens. Another version says that there was a Sir John Helyon
who married the heiress to the estate.

In the early fourteenth century the house came into the ownership of Lord Audley, through marriage with Yseult Mortimer,
widow of Walter de Batun. Yseult's brother was Roger Mortimer,
who, with his mistress, Isabella, Queen of England, ousted her
husband, Edward II from the throne and had him imprisoned
and eventually murdered in Berkeley Castle in 1327. A few days
before the King was captured, Mortimer brought the Queen and
her son, the future Edward III, then fourteen years old, to Much
Marcle, confident of a welcome from Mortimer's sister, Yseult.
After Edward III came to the throne, he took revenge on his
father's persecutors and their supporters, and Yseult and her
husband thought it wise to leave the estate to the care of Walter
Helyon and disappear from the neighbourhood. Years after
Roger Mortimer's execution, Yseult, then a widow, did return to

Hellens. Her relationship with King Edward was apparently good, for his son Edward, known as the Black Prince, became a lifelong friend from his boyhood with her grandson, James Audley, who fought with the Prince at Crécy. In the Court Room of Hellens, James erected a massive fireplace, decorated with the Prince of Wales' feathers, in readiness for a visit by the Black Prince, when he stayed a night on a journey from Chester to Hereford. James was eventually killed in battle and left no heir, so the estate came to another branch of the family by the female line. Few ancient houses have had such a continuous occupation from their construction to the present day, for Hellens has never been sold out of the family.

Few houses, too, have had so many royal personages passing through its doors: Edward II's Queen, her son the future Edward III and his son, the Black Prince. There is a legend that Mary Tudor, Queen of England, slept at Hellens, and so we have 'the Queen's Room', where the Queen's portcullis badge and her initials appear over the fire place. Little wonder that, with such a history, Hellens has its ghost – not a royal ghost but that of a Roman Catholic priest or monk who served the religious needs of the Walwyn family, who, in their turn, inherited the estate by marriage to the heiress. The priest, it is said, was discovered by the Roundheads and killed in the house, and from this story we have the 'Monk's Walk' and the 'Monk's Sleeping Place', as the dovecote is called, in the grounds, just outside the house.

This octagonal brick building, decorated conspicuously with the date 1641 and the large white letter F and M, adjoins the herb garden, divided into various shapes by low bush hedges where the house cat likes to laze in the sun. The letters F and M stand for Fulke Walwyn, who in 1641 married his guardian's daughter Margaret, when they were both teenagers. Their marriage was short-lived, as in the following year Fulke joined the Royalist forces in the Civil War and, at the head of his retainers, passed through the gate we see beyond the gardens. The gate was erected in 1641 across a drive which no longer exists and is still known as the 'new gate', looking onto an open field. The young man never returned to Hellens, and the gate is said to have remained closed ever since. Margaret gave birth to Fulke's son, John, about the time the Cromwellian troops raided the house, killing the old family chaplain in one of the bedrooms, and the family fled to Hereford. The marks reputed to be bullet holes and signs of battering on the front door are said to be the results of that raid.

As for Fulke, after unsuccessful battles he is believed to have gone into hiding and made a living as a snow-sweeper in Hereford, only to die just as the Restoration of the Monarchy was announced. Hellens was returned to his son, John.

It is an interesting fact that in the 1984 television serial *By the Sword Divided*, which told of similar events, Hellens was used for certain outdoor scenes, such as the arrival of the fugitive King Charles II. However, this incident did not take place at Hellens but at Leigh Court on the outskirts of Bristol, where Charles arrived disguised as a manservant of Jane Lane, a cousin of Mrs Norton, who with her husband, George Norton, owned the Court. Although the Nortons did not recognize him, the old butler did, but he was a good Royalist and passed him off to the soldiers as a kitchenboy.

Hellens is not one of those imposing mansions of classic design with an impressive staircase leading up to an enormous door, the house surrounded by extensive landscaped grounds with vistas, lakes, grottoes and temple. With its low, warm red-brick Jacobean front and homely door, it seems to invite you inside. It has no extensive park but attractive gardens adjoining the house, with small ponds and flowerbeds, enhanced by statuettes and animal figures. In fact, it is not a museum but a house for living in. It is not, of course, all Jacobean. Some parts are Tudor and some are older, as the lower courses of some of the walls show.

The usual way into the house is through an arch into a small courtyard. The arch was partly destroyed by a bomb during the last war but has been restored in brick, and the original Audley coat of arms has been rescued and reinstated. The building to the left of the courtyard was also damaged and has been rebuilt with battlements according to an old plan. From the courtyard we enter the Court Room, with a minstrel gallery, a stone flag floor and a refectory table made from a massive altar top, with consecration crosses marked on it. In front of the fireplace are two chairs of similar pattern, except that one has arms and seat a little higher than the other. The story is that these were made for the visit of the Tudor Queen Mary, who would have sat on the higher chair as became her rank. This hall would have been the banqueting room and is known as the Court Room because at Hellens was held the Courts Baron, an assembly which dealt with Manorial disputes.

A Jacobean staircase, which presumably was installed as an

advantage over the older stone newel staircase in the staircase tower, leads to the upper floor. Its side panelling is carved with winged wyverns, their tails lashed together with a ring. The winged wyvern was incorporated into the Walwyn crest, and it has been suggested that the ring symbolizes the marriage of Fulke and Margaret.

One of the rooms on the first floor is 'Poor Hetty's Room', where Hetty Walwyn was kept in seclusion for her dreadful sin of falling in love and running away with one of her father's labourers. Hetty's portrait on the wall of the room seems to have captured the unhappy expression as though Hetty foresaw her fate. A bellrope hangs in this small room. Did Hetty have to use this to call a servant when needed? The rope still operates the bell in the tower above, and some people say they can still sense the sadness in the room.

On the first floor, too, is the Cordova Room, so called because of the wallcovering of Cordova leather. Then there is the Queen's Room, so named because Mary Tudor is said to have slept there. Hellens is certainly a house worth visiting.

Close to Hellens is Mortimer's Castle, not a castle in the usual sense but a Norman motte and bailey. It was the forerunner of Hellens, the site of the first of the castles at Much Marcle. Opposite Hellens are St Bartholomew's Church and the resting places of some of those who have lived in the old house. A fascinating tomb is that of Blanche Mortimer, Yseult's sister, who became Lady Grandison. Her husband, Sir Peter Grandison, outlived her, and his monument is in Hereford Cathedral where there is an Audley Chapel. Blanche's effigy is a remarkable piece of sculpture. The beautiful face is rendered naturally, and her dress hangs over one corner of the tomb chest in a most realistic fashion. When originally painted, it must have looked even more lifelike. Blanche's tomb can be seen just as you enter the church, and nearby are the iron gates to the chapel which has, in the centre, a tomb chest with a pair of figures of about 1400. That of the woman also has touches of realism, such as the puppies which pull at her skirt. Perhaps the most unusual effigy in the church is that of a man, dating to the second half of the fourteenth century. It is one of those rare carvings of oak, important enough to have been shown with other outstanding items at a special exhibition in London in 1971. It is said to represent Walter Helyon, the steward who took over Hellens, or Sir John Helyon, who is said to have gone on a pilgrimage to the Holy Land and come back with medical knowledge which he used to cure men and animals alike. The story is that the grateful parishioners carried his effigy round the church each harvest festival, and this practice continued until 1649.

In the churchyard, close to the church porch, is a yew so large that its hollow trunk has been fitted with seating sufficient for seven people. Its great branches, supported on a circular framework, form a fine shaded area around the tree. The name Marcle is derived from 'march', meaning a border region, and Much means 'big', quite a common adjective in the place names of the district.

A couple of miles to the north-west of Much Marcle is Marcle Hill, and at the north end of the ridge the Ordnance Survey map is marked with the site of the 'Wonder Landslip AD 1575'. Camden described the incident in the flowery language of his day as follows: 'A hill which they call Marcle Hill in the year 1575 roused itself, as it were, out of sleep, and for three days together, shoving its prodigious body forwards with a horrible roaring noise and overturning all that stood in its way, advanced itself to the astonishment of all beholders, to a higher station, by that kind of earthquake the which the naturalists call Brosmatia.' You will not find that word in many dictionaries today, as the simple word is 'landslip'. The usual cause of landslips, like that of Marcle Hill, is unstable rock sliding along an inclined bed of clay.

The way back to the Wye is through Woolhope, a mile to the west. Although a long way from Coventry, a modern window in St George's Church features Lady Godiva, or Godgifu, and her sister Wuliva. A small quatrefoil window at the top shows Godiva on her white horse, and below are two long windows, that on the right showing her standing, holding a tabby cat and with a grey dog at her feet and that on the left Wuliva with a dog. The sisters are connected with Woolhope because they are said to have owned the manor which they presented to the diocese and Hereford Cathedral in the eleventh century. In fact, the name Woolhope has been suggested as a contraction of 'Wuliva's Hope', a 'hope' being an enclosed valley or hollow in the side of a hill. The word is common in place-names in the district and also in Derbyshire.

The Woolhope district is known as an interesting geological area, with quite a variety of rocks and fossils. It even has its own limestone, Woolhope Limestone, the Woolhope Dome in geological language. Needless to say, Woolhope has evolved its own Naturalists' Field Club, founded in 1854 to study not only geology but other aspects of natural history as well.

It was a past president of the club who introduced the original ley-line theory. Alfred Watkins, born in 1855, in his late sixties gave the first talk on his theory to the Woolhope Naturalists' Field Club, followed within a few years by his book *The Old Straight Track*. The basis of the theory is that many ancient monuments and old churches are in line, although there may be considerable distances between them. It is reasonable enough to assume that many ancient monuments now remotely situated adjoined tracks, and indeed there must have been a whole network of walking or riding tracks all over the country. In Roman times some were converted into more substantial roads, but many have long since disappeared. Subsequently the theory has been developed to suggest that these tracks or ley lines were along natural 'force' lines, and this in fact is the reason for their position and for the erection of monuments along them. In recent years, a television programme showed that in some cases at least such a force appeared to be registered. However, since Watkins wrote his book, certain esoteric significance has been added to the study of these lost tracks, and suggestions have been made that they could be landing-strips for UFOs or even 'dragon tracks'. Watkins was an excellent photographer, and much of his work is in Hereford Museum. In his earlier days he was the inventor of a photographic lightmeter and became a fellow of the Royal Photographic Society.

Two miles south-west is Fownhope, near the east bank of the Wye. This was a port of call for pleasure and cargo boats making their way to Ross and Chepstow. In 1819 the crew of three were drowned at Fownhope when their coal barge capsized. In 1905 a project was under consideration to raise the river by 4½ feet, so that steam vessels could travel between Belmont and Fownhope. There were strong objections from the salmon fishermen, and the scheme was dropped. The river shallows have always been a problem on the Wye, and a number of weirs were constructed, finally to disappear.

The attractive timber-framed building is the 'Green Man', once called the 'Naked Boy', and is dated to 1485. The interior is as fascinating as the outside, with its timbering and uneven ceiling and walls. At one end of the timbered dining-room, an extensive mural depicts various events which took place in Fownhope. The picture includes a judge and a prisoner being led

Fownhope church

away, from the time when the inn was used as a court and a temporary prison. There are also a coach and horses, a reference to the use of the premises as a staging post between Hereford and Gloucester, a trooper, a pugilist and various people from Fownhope's past. The pugilist represents Tom Spring, who was a bare-fist prizefighter before the days of boxing-gloves. He was born in Fownhope and became the English champion. The trooper is a reminder of the Civil War, when Cromwell's troops, under Colonel Birch, spent the night in Fownhope on their way from besieging Goodrich to attacking Hereford.

Charles II is also remembered in the 'Club Walk', an annual event on the Saturday on or nearest 6/7 June, commemorating the day Charles II entered London for the Restoration of 1660. It is called the 'Club Walk' because members of the Fownhope Hearts of Oak Society parade through the street carrying club-like sticks, decorated with flowers.

Fownhope is mainly an agricultural and a commuter village for Hereford but once had quite a bit of industry, particularly in connection with the river trade. Bark-stripping to supply bark for tanning, lime-production, building, rope-making and brewing were among its occupations; there were, of course, local village craftsmen, such as the blacksmith and saddler, and many more shops within the village. This was, of course, true of many villages before the manufacture of articles became more centralized and communications improved. Reminders of the past are the village stocks on the main road, recessed into the churchyard wall.

The church has a broach spire on a Norman tower, and the interior has a range of architectural styles from Norman or Romanesque to fifteenth-century work. The extremely well-preserved Norman tympanum, supported on brackets on a wall inside the church, is a good example of the Herefordshire School of Norman sculpture. Usually at the head of a doorway leading into the church, its original location is unknown. It was possibly removed during an early restoration of the church and rebuilt on the outside of the west wall, to be removed in modern times into the church. The central figure is the Virgin Mary, and the long parallel folds of her dress and other details are typical of the Herefordshire style. The coils of ribbon decoration are reminiscent of, but not identical with, Saxon work. This motif still persisted to some extent into Norman times, as Saxon workmen still carried out much of the work. As it is not easy to draw a hard line between late Saxon and early Norman design, both styles are now included in the general term 'Romanesque'.

Some two miles towards Hereford, on the junction of the Wye and the Lugg, is Mordiford, where there are great tales about a dragon which used to harass the neighbourhood until it was destroyed by a condemned criminal named Garnstone or Garston. He was guaranteed his freedom if he rid the people of Mordiford of the monster. He did so by hiding in a barrel and shooting at the dragon through the bunghole, but his freedom came only through death, for the barrel caught fire from the dragon's burning breath, so unlike St George poor Garnstone never lived to enjoy his reward. He did, however, have his memorial, not inside the church but outside, where for many years a twelve-foot-long green dragon with forked tongue and red mouth was painted on the gable of the church, with the following inscription:

> This is a true effigy of the strange
> Prodigious monster, which our wood did range.
> In Eastwood it by Garnstone's hand was slayne
> A truth which old mythologists maintain.

The effigy went when alterations were made to the church in 1811. However, a picture of it can be seen within the church and also in Hereford Museum.

As to the origin of the dragon, this was described by J. Dacres Devlin in 1848 in *Helps to Hereford History*. According to his account, Maude, a young girl, was blackberry-picking when in one of the bushes she found a small green creature, about the size of a cucumber, with bright eyes, slender tail and wings. It was such a pretty little thing that she took a fancy to it and took it home. Her parents were sure it was evil and proposed to kill it, so she hid it in the barn. One day, tired of Maude's saucers of milk, it escaped and grew and grew, killing cattle and even attacking people.

Why did the story of the dragon arise in the first place? The manor of Mordiford was once owned by St Cuthlac's priory at Hereford. The priory coat of arms is described as 'gules [red] a wyvern passant [walking] wings displayed and tail'. Could these arms have given rise to the Mordiford dragon and could the dragon story be linked with the noise made by the great landslip of 1575 on Marcle Hill? There is still a lane called 'Serpent's Lane' where no grass is said to grow and where the dragon stalked its prey.

Mordiford has suffered not only from dragons but from what is more authenticated – floods, now alleviated by recent drainage works, though farmers have mixed opinions about the works, as moderate floods brought valuable silt which improved the soil. A defaced stone tablet in the church records that

> . . . at Mordiford May 1811, between the hours of five and nine p.m. the village . . . was visited by a tremendous storm of thunder, lightning and wind and rain by which the little river Pentaloe was swollen in some places to an extent of one hundred and eighty feet in width to a depth of twenty feet.
>
> Just above the said village – the road leading to Woolhope many hundreds of tons of rock were blown up and carried through the said village, by which several of the houses of the inhabitants were much injured and the gardens nearly destroyed.
>
> A subscription was promoted for the principal sufferers and a sum of £80 was collected and distributed amongst them in proportion to their respective losses.

The bridge at Mordiford has nine arches and is probably fourteenth-century with sixteenth-century alteration. The lords of Mordiford in Norman times held the manor subject to presenting the king with a pair of golden spurs whenever he crossed the bridge.

Holme Lacy, across the Wye and south-west of Mordiford, was once the home of an influential family, the Scudamores, some of whom are buried in the church there. Holme Lacy House, probably the largest in Herefordshire, was built by the second Viscount Scudamore in 1675, soon after his marriage, but probably not completed until 1680, as some of the magnificent plaster ceilings date to that time. It also had some exceptionally fine woodwork by Grinling Gibbons, but some was taken to another and present-day home of the Scudamores, Kentchurch Court, near Grosmont Castle on the River Monnow, and some of it is in New York. In modern times Holme Lacy has been used as a nursing home but it has now been empty for a number of years. It still contains a number of seventeenth-century features, including the fine ceilings, but when Sir Robert Lucas Tooth bought it in 1909, he made extensive alterations. However, in 1920 he sold it, and four years later it was resold to one of the Wills family, who eventually presented the house and some adjoining land to the Herefordshire County Council.

The present house replaces a former house of the thirteenth century built by the Lacys, who gave the house its name and who came over with William the Conqueror. In the fourteenth century they were succeeded by the Scudamores, and in this old house lived the first Viscount Scudamore; Charles I was entertained there in 1645. To the Scudamores, Herefordshire is indebted to two of the most famous products of the county, its Herefordshire cattle and its cider.

The church of St Cuthbert, near the riverbank about a mile from the house, is indeed a mausoleum of the Scudamores, judging by the large number of tombs and monumental tablets to that family, ranging from the late sixteenth to the late nineteenth century. It was during a visit to Holme Lacy that Alexander Pope is believed to have written part of his *Moral Essays* concerning John Kyrle whom he called 'the Man of Ross' (p. 160–3).

Dinedor Hill lies between Holme Lacy and Hereford. Here is Dinedor Hill Fort, one of those Iron Age defences consisting of banks and ditches which crown many hills. In pre-Roman times they were defences against turbulent neighbours and in some cases became fortresses against the Roman invaders. Until recent years they were thought to be merely places of defence to which people could flee with their goods and animals when an enemy approached, but not for permanent habitation. In some cases traces of habitation have been found within the banks, as at Dinedor, where a quantity of Iron Age and Romano-British pottery was found. Years ago, when Dr Mortimer Wheeler excavated Maiden Castle Hill fort at Dorset, he concluded that it had been occupied as an Iron Age town, but the idea that the forts were for defence and not occupation remained until the present time. In recent years more excavation has been carried out within the banks of some hill-forts, and in the comparatively few cases which have been examined it now seems that they were occupied permanently. Perhaps Wheeler's interpretation of the 'city' of Maiden Castle was not so far off the truth.

Across the Wye from Dinedor is Hampton Bishop, where St Andrew's Church contains some interesting Norman work, particularly the south doorway, the chancel and the northern chapel arches, and the remains of a stone reredos of the fifteenth century, something of a rarity. There are also some picturesque old houses and an inn with a curious name, the Bunch of Carrots, down by the river. It is a quiet village, with a rural atmosphere, although we are nearly into the City of Hereford.

11

Hereford

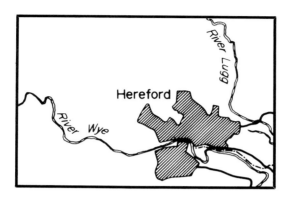

Hereford is a busy market town with a thriving shopping centre and considerable traffic problems. It is well known for its weekly cattle market, held on Wednesdays, not only for its famous cattle, but for other livestock, sheep and pigs. It is the biggest gathering of country people for many miles around, as I found when I visited or tried to visit the market on market day. There was a great influx of vehicles of every description, lorries, cattle trucks, vans, large cars and little cars, all trying to get in or get out of the parking area. In the end I gave it up, resolving to get there earlier next time.

One of the principal events in Hereford is the May Fair, now held during the second week in May in the City centre and adjoining streets. Originally it was known as St Ethelbert's Fair, when a royal grant was made to the Bishop of Hereford by Henry I to hold a three day fair, later extended to nine days. Such royal grants were common during the twelfth century, usually in return for payments to the King, well worth while for the privileges of exacting tolls on incoming goods at the city gates and for booth rentals.

The May Fair still survives, but no longer as the Bishop's fair, for in 1838, by Act of Parliament, the Corporation purchased the Bishop's rights by payment of twelve and a half bushels of wheat or its money value. This corn rent was paid until 1980 when the

The Old House, Hereford

Hereford Cathedral

City reintroduced the old custom of payment in wheat. Twelve and a half bushels of sacked wheat are brought to the official opening and presented by the Mayor to the Bishop. To ensure that the payment is just, one of the sacks is emptied into a bushel measure, borrowed from the City Museum, and there is an official speech, declaring the fair open. For three days High Town, Broad Street, Commercial Street and King Street are closed to traffic and, as it often rains, local people refer to the rain at this time as 'May Fair weather'.

The fair today has greatly changed since medieval times. Manufactured goods are on the stalls and the old entertainment of acrobats, wrestlers and medieval games have been replaced by the modern fun fair. The city gates and their tolls have disappeared and the laden mules, carts and pedlars have given way to motorized transport.

From the congested roads, Hereford shows none of the atmosphere of a cathedral city. You have to explore on foot, discovering and savouring the mixture of old and new, the alleyways, the pedestrian precincts, the quiet oasis of the cathedral and the river walks. It was an ancient city, once the capital of Saxon Mercia, and is believed to have taken its name from a ford across the Wye, the 'army ford'. This was the place where an army could always cross and the usual place for anyone to cross the river until a wooden bridge was built during the twelfth century. When the bridge was washed away, Richard II gave wood and stone for its repair and granted Hereford the right to collect tolls for twenty years on goods being brought across the bridge. The present Wye Bridge was built in 1490 and the single-span concrete Greyfriars Bridge in 1965.

An interesting approach to the city is a walk through the Bishop's Meadow and King George's Field. On reaching the river, you cross the Wye by a pretty iron footbridge, erected to commemorate Queen Victoria's Diamond Jubilee. On a sunny day, there is a fine view of the cathedral reflected in the water. At the other end of the bridge, mount the steps by a bastion and walk through Castle Green to the cathedral precincts. Castle Green is now a wide, open park and in the centre, by some colourful flowerbeds, is a column commemorating Nelson. Here was the great castle of Hereford, built as a protection against the Welsh raids. Although in some disrepair, the castle played its part in the Civil War until it was taken over by Colonel Birch in 1646, to be demolished in 1652 and the stone sold. Part of the moat still exists but has been landscaped to form a pleasant feature. Near here is St Ethelbert's Well, said to have miraculous healing powers, particularly for sores. This is where the body of the murdered saint rested for a while on his last journey to Hereford Cathedral for re-burial, and a healing spring sprang from the spot.

On the way to the cathedral, we pass some charming old buildings, including one black-and-white house, with a small barrel suspended over the front door. It received an award for its excellent restoration and is now the school tuckshop. Then comes the Cathedral School and we pass into the precincts of the cathedral.

Hereford was established as a cathedral city about AD 700. Putta, Bishop of Rochester, who had suffered the loss of his own cathedral burnt by raiders, is reputed to have been given land here for a new cathedral and became the first bishop. It was rebuilt by Bishop Athelstan early in the eleventh century. However, Hereford was very much a border town and in 1055 was sacked by the Welsh, who burnt the cathedral and killed seven of the canons. The present cathedral was begun by the Normans soon after the Conquest.

The cathedral has two unique treasures, the Mappa Mundi, a late thirteenth- or early fourteenth-century map of the world, and a chained library.

The Mappa Mundi is shown in a wall frame opposite the spiral staircase of fifty-four stairs leading up to the chained library. The coloured map on calf vellum is about five feet six inches wide and four feet six inches deep. The world is shown as a circle with Jerusalem in the middle and *Britannia Insula*, the British Isles, almost over the edge of the world in the bottom left-hand corner. The map contains a wealth of material, both written and drawn, much of it from information in the Bible but also a great deal from other sources. It is surprising how much information Richard de Bello, a prebendary in the cathedral, managed to get onto his map – or his '*estoire*', a history or story, as he called it. Here are the 'Wie' and 'Hford', and not only many rivers and towns of the British Isles but cities and geographical features throughout the then known world. As would be expected with an ancient map, much of the information is incorrectly shaped and inaccurate, but this adds to its interest, showing the medieval scholars' view of the world. Incorporated into it are the familiar 'doom' pictures, an angel calling the righteous from their graves and another condemning the damned to the jaws of Hell.

It is the oldest and largest map of its kind in the world, only surpassed in size and probably slightly in date by the German Ebstorf map which was destroyed in the Second World War. Fortunately there are copies of both maps, and a copy of the German map is kept in the cathedral. During the last war the Mappa Mundi was deposited in a mine for safety. When it was returned to the cathedral after the end of the war, it was mounted in its present frame, made from wood recovered from bombed London churches.

The 'chained library' is a small room with a series of shelves placed at right angles containing ancient books chained to bars. Along one wall are showcases with some of the most important works. Among the ancient Bibles in the library is the 'Cider' Bible, so called because the words 'strong drink' in this version were replaced by 'cider'. Some eighth-century manuscripts are among the most valuable possessions, and also on display is a Hereford prayer-book, missing for 300 years until it was purchased from a secondhand-bookseller in Drury Lane, London.

Rare as chained libraries are, Hereford has two. The other and much smaller library is in All Saints' Church in the High Street. This is the church where the actor David Garrick was baptized in 28 February 1716, probably in the present fourteenth-century font. All Saints' Library was a bequest of 1715. The chaining system of the books is similar to that in the cathedral, and the books include a 'Breeches' Bible – in which Adam and Eve sew fig leaves together to make 'breeches'. An example, opened at the appropriate page, can be seen in the Old House in a showcase on the ground floor.

Monasteries often had two libraries, one for the general use of the monks and one where rare books were kept, which were not intended to be removed. They were often protected from theft by being stored in wooden chests, but later there were chained libraries, a system followed by cathedrals, some churches and even ancient municipal libraries. Many of the books are gifts of bishops, and Bishop Athelstan, who died in 1056, is believed to have donated the pre-Conquest copy of the four Gospels. In the present bookcases, which date to 1611, each book is secured by a chain running along a horizontal bar, each chain being sufficiently long to enable the book to be withdrawn and opened on the reading-shelf. Although the present 1,500 volumes make the cathedral's chained library the largest in England, Hereford also has the second largest, that at All Saints' Church, with a mere 313 volumes. The cathedral library was originally housed in the old west cloister and later in the Lady Chapel, while its present room used to house the treasury.

In a corner of the chained library in the cathedral is displayed the wooden leg of an effigy. To find its source you must descend the fifty-four steps to the floor of the cathedral and seek out the tomb effigy of Richard de Pembridge, who died in 1375. His effigy, like several in the cathedral, was mutilated during the Civil War and poor Richard lost a leg. It was subsequently replaced by a wooden one, carved with a second garter to match the other leg, until such time as a more permanent limb was fixed and the wooden leg was superfluous. His fingers remain broken.

There are quite a number of interesting effigies in the cathedral. One is that of Bishop Booth, who died in 1535, another of Johanna de Bohun, Countess of Hereford, who died in 1327, and one of Peter de Grandison, who died in 1352. There is Robert Bennet, who held office in the cathedral from 1602 to 1617 and, like many, offended Queen Elizabeth I but regained favour and was appointed Dean of Windsor. He was a great tennis-player. There is the man whose keys are at his side to indicate that he was a chancellor at the cathedral. Another effigy is that of Geoffrey de Clive, bishop from 1115 to 1119, a member of the family from which Robert Clive, founder of the Indian Empire, was descended, some 600 years later. An unusually graffiti-covered effigy is that of John Henley, who was precentor from 1489 to 1491 and dean until his death in 1500: there is hardly a space on the alabaster between the numerous scratches and names, while the dates 1657 and 1862 are clearly visible. An effigy of an earlier precentor is that of John Swinfield, who held office in the late thirteenth and early fourteenth centuries. His feet rest not on a dog or even on a lion but on a pig, a rebus or pun on the first four letters of his name. The surrounding arch is decorated with a series of pigs and acorns.

The marble effigy and tomb of John Stanbury, who was bishop from 1453 to 1474, is opposite his small ornate chantry chapel, built a few years after his death. He was confessor to King Henry VI and was involved with the King in establishing Eton College. The monarch invited him to be its first provost, but he declined and was offered the bishopric of Hereford instead.

The Saxon and the medieval cathedrals of Hereford were the burial-places of two saints, Ethelbert and Thomas de Cantilupe.

Hereford Cathedral from the north-east

In fact, the cathedral is dedicated to the Virgin Mary and St Ethelbert. King of East Anglia, Ethelbert was contracted to marry the daughter of Offa, King of Mercia, and in spite of evil omens and dreams of blood travelled to Mercia to claim his bride. He was apparently well received at Offa's palace, believed to have been at Sutton Walls, just north of Hereford, but Offa determined upon his death – some say he wanted to add Ethelbert's kingdom to his own and some that Offa's queen, outraged at Ethelbert's resistance to her amorous advances, persuaded her husband to have him murdered. The unsuspecting Ethelbert came before Offa, leaving his sword behind, and was seized and beheaded. Legend goes on to say that his body was brought down the hill to Marden for burial, and Offa, in expiation of the crime, later built a church on the site. There is still a holy well in the church where a healing spring arose when Ethelbert's body was removed from Marden and carried to the Saxon cathedral of Hereford for reburial about 793. I was told that St Ethelbert's well at Marden is now dry, but when I saw it recently, there was certainly water in it.

St Thomas de Cantilupe, born in Buckinghamshire, became

Bishop of Hereford in 1275 and died in Italy in 1282 on his way to protest to the Pope about his quarrel with the Archbishop of Canterbury. His heart was buried in his monastery at Ashbridge in his native Buckinghamshire, but his bones were brought back to Hereford to be buried in the Lady Chapel of the cathedral. Miracles were reported at his shrine, and many pilgrims began to visit it in search of cures. In 1287, because of the lack of space for the multitude who flocked to his tomb, his bones were placed in the north transept in a reliquary where they could be seen and carried in procession on religious occasions. In 1349 the remains were moved back to the Lady Chapel, but although the empty shrine still remains in the north transept, there is now no trace of the tomb or the bones in the Lady Chapel, for these were lost in the destruction following the Reformation.

There were stories that one of the cathedral priests had managed to retrieve the skull. In 1672 an English Benedictine lay brother visited his sister near Hereford and found that she had the skull. He took it back to his monastery at Lambspring in Germany. This monastery closed in 1802 and the monastic church, where the skull had been sealed into the wall behind the altar, became the parish church. There it remained until 1882, when another Benedictine brother recovered it after a search and brought it back to his own monastery at Downside Abbey in north Somerset.

A church which still possesses a reliquary is the Roman Catholic church of St Francis Xavier in Broad Street. The reliquary, against the wall on the right side of the altar, contains the hand of John Kemble, the eighty-year-old priest hanged in the late seventeenth century for his supposed implication in the Popish Plot. His body was dismembered after the hanging, and the hand was retrieved. Was it the same hand that held the 'Kemble Pipe', a local saying meaning 'one for the road'? The story is that at his execution John Kemble asked for time to say his prayers and finish his pipe. The request was granted and then the under-sheriff asked for time to finish his pipe, to which John Kemble agreed. St Francis Xavier's church, built in 1838–9, is very much the classic design of the period, with steps, columns and pediment, after the style of the Treasury of the Athenians at Delphi, but narrower. It is the kind of structure which should stand alone and not shoulder to shoulder with other buildings. Inside, the building is lofty and without aisles, producing an impression of space.

A descendant of the same family as the priest was Roger Kemble, head of a family of strolling players. He was born in Hereford in 1721 and married another player, Sarah Wood. They had twelve children, some of whom became players, and the one of everlasting fame was named after her mother after marriage becoming Sarah Siddons, said to haunt the Theatre Royal in Bristol. She was born in Brecon during a visit there by the family, whose children were inevitably born in various places. Sarah Kemble married another player in her father's company, much to the annoyance of her parents, who had their eye on someone better, a well-established farmer, and Siddons was a very in-different actor; the only outstanding address he ever made on the public stage was the attack he made on Mrs Kemble for standing between her daughter and himself. It brought down the house and raised Mrs Kemble's ire. He did not make a good husband and was dependent on his wife's fame and fortune. There was a Kemble Theatre in Hereford, but it closed down in the 1960s.

Hereford seems to have had strong connections with the theatre, as David Garrick was born there in 1717, although he spent much of his life in London. His birthplace is believed to have stood on the corner of Widemarsh Street and Maylord Street but has now been demolished. However, perhaps Hereford's most colourful theatrical personality was Nell Gwynne (or Gwyn) who, it is claimed, was born in a house in what is now known as Nell Gwynne Street, originally Pipe Lane. A plaque on the street's boundary wall indicates the site of her birthplace, although some believe she was born near Drury Lane, London, in 1651. Her father was of Welsh origin, hence her surname, and the family may well have originated in Herefordshire, for there were many Welsh people in the old Archenfield corner and many came into Hereford from Wales itself, as indeed they do today.

Nell became an actress at fifteen and played a number of leading roles. Pepys, in his diary entry of 25 March 1667, spoke very highly of her performance, and Dryden provided her with many of her parts. Her last theatre appearance was in 1670 in Dryden's *Conquest of Granada*, a two-part tragedy. Nell was short, with reddish hair, and her high spirits appealed to the populace and no doubt to Charles II. She and the King remained lovers until his death in 1685, when she was thirty-four and he fifty-five. Nell survived him by less than three years and was buried in St Martin's in the Fields, London. James II paid her debts and provided her with an estate which passed on her death to the

Duke of St Albans, one of her two sons by Charles. So James II honoured his brother's dying request, 'Let not poor Nelly starve.' She was always illiterate, able only to scrawl her own initials 'E.G.' (Eleanor Gwyn). She never dabbled in politics, was generous and is said to have persuaded Charles to found the Chelsea Hospital for retired soldiers. It is interesting to note that the uniform of the Chelsea Pensioners is similar to that of the pensioners of Coningsby Hospital in Widemarsh Street and perhaps, if indeed she was a Hereford girl, she may have suggested the same uniform for Chelsea Hospital. Nell's grandson, Lord James Beauclerk, was one of the bishops of Hereford.

Thomas Traherne, son of a Hereford shoemaker, was a writer and poet. His works were of a religious nature, and at one time he was a rector at Credenhill, Hereford. His poems and a religious work were found in a bookshop in 1896 or 1897 and were thought by one authority to have been the work of Henry Vaughan the seventeenth-century Welsh mystic poet but were later established as that of Thomas Traherne, who died in 1674.

John Bull, a seventeenth-century organist and composer, born of a Somerset family, once served as an organist at Hereford but later became one of the organists of James I. After acting as organist in many places on the Continent, he died at Antwerp in 1688, where he was the cathedral organist. Britain's national anthem is attributed to an 'ayre' written by John Bull in 1619, but this is a controversial point as several other composers have been credited with it. He was not connected with the cartoon character personifying England.

A composer of modern times, Sir Edward Elgar, known for many works including *Pomp and Circumstance*, lived in Hereford for a time, arriving in 1904, and it was even suggested in 1905 that he should become mayor. It is said that he declined the honour as he was a Roman Catholic and as mayor he would be expected to attend the cathedral on occasions, in his official capacity. In fact, he did go to the cathedral from time to time, particularly when his own works were performed. He also went to Gloucester and Worcester, the other two cathedrals where the Three-Choirs Festival is held, a festival which officially dates from about 1724. Its first performance was in Gloucester, but the idea came from the Chancellor of Hereford, the Reverend Thomas Bisse, as a means of raising funds to help widows and orphans of needy clergy of all three dioceses. Although Elgar lived in Hereford for only about eight years, quite a number of his works were written

View of the Wye upstream, Tintern

in Hereford, so no wonder the city is proud of the self-taught musician, the son of a Worcester piano-tuner. Elgar in his turn was fond of Hereford and of fishing in the Wye.

Going back a few centuries, there was one notable person who came unwillingly to Hereford, and that was the grandfather of Henry VII, Owen Tudor, who was beheaded by the Yorkists in Hereford market-place in 1461. Part of the ancient market-place is now a pedestrian precinct but the butter market is still there, with stalls selling local products. This area is called High Town, but the precinct, with its seating and paving, is reminiscent of a great Continental *place*. It used to be a busy traffic intersection and now it is still very busy, particularly on market days, but only with foot traffic. At one end stands what is believed to be the oldest house in Hereford, the Old House.

Three storeys high and gabled with decorated bargeboards and overhanging upper floors, the Old House was built in 1621. It is a typical timber-framed house of the period and was once part of 'Butchers' Row' but probably looks more splendid in its isolation. It is now a museum and furnished in seventeenth-century style.

The internal timbering and sloping floors are as fascinating as the outside, and on the top floor a glass insertion in the ceiling gives a view of the roof timbering. One of the ground-floor ceilings has some fine plaster decoration.

In the larger of the two ground-floor rooms is a painting, artist unknown, of Sir Henry and Lady Lingen. It was Sir Henry who held Goodrich Castle for the King, was besieged by the Parliamentarian army and survived to become Member of Parliament for Hereford. Some idea of old Herefordshire is given by models of several market houses in the surrounding areas, buildings on piers, such as those found at Ross and Ledbury, where the market was held beneath the main structure out of the worst of the weather. One model is of the old Market House in Hereford itself, a fine building which once stood on part of what is now the pedestrian precinct. On the upper floors is a wealth of carved wooden bedroom furniture, including four-poster beds. A small carved plaque, 'The Lawsuit', is a comment on the processes of law: one man is pulling a cow by its head, another by its tail, while the lawyer sits in the middle, milking the animal. Part of the

The Preaching Cross, Coningsby Hospital, Hereford

original mural on one of the walls is protected under glass, as are some others from old Hereford buildings.

In spite of the small window-panes, the interior is well lit, and the room affords a view of the people in High Town, hurrying or sauntering across the old market-place or resting on the seats enjoying a sunny morning. The Old House was once the premises of the Butchers' Guild. In recent times it was a branch of Lloyds Bank, who presented it to the city.

The public library and museum, built 1872–4, are in Broad Street, a good example of Victorian Gothic with ornate carvings and embellishments, the type of building erected at that time for museums and art galleries in many British towns. The exhibits themselves seem to take second place to the overwhelming architecture and elaborate settings. Between the wars, the fashion for stark buildings and plain furniture seems to have benefited at least museum collections, for they now shine forth against the unobtrusive and often unlit background of the modern museum. In Hereford the public library occupies the ground floor and the museum and art gallery the first floor. On the staircase are mosaics from the Roman town of Magna at Kenchester. In the gallery are specimens and plans from excavations and a skeleton arm, said to be that of St Ursula, and in the inner rooms is a fine collection of Oriental ceramics.

In Widemarsh Street is the St John Medieval Museum in the Coningsby Hospital, one of the most historic sites in Hereford. The Dominicans ('black friars') had a monastery at the rear in the fourteenth century. Now all that remains of the monastic buildings are an empty, roofless shell and the tall, elaborate, hexagonal friars' preaching cross with its narrow gallery mounted by steps. Most of these friars' preaching crosses were destroyed, and this is believed to be the only remaining one in the country. The Knights Hospitallers of St John of Jerusalem had their house and hostelry there, dating back to the thirteenth century, but in 1614 Sir Thomas Coningsby decided to establish his hospital or almshouse for old compaigners and retired servants there, making use of what was left of the walls and chapel when he built the attractive quadrangle and buildings around it today. There were eleven poor inmates from Hereford and adjoining counties, six of whom had to be old soldiers who had served in wars for at least three years, or old sailors, and the remaining five were old menservants who had served the same family for at least seven years. The inmate chosen as the head of the establishment was known as the 'corporal', assisted by a chaplain.

Today you pass through the gatehouse from busy Widemarsh Street to a quadrangle with grass and flowers, a pleasant retreat, with ancient tenements on three sides and the hall and chapel on the north side. On the far side of the quadrangle a passageway leads to the ruins of the monastic site. The double-storeyed hall is now a museum, giving a picture of the hospital's history, with tableaux of wax figures in period costume, including a Knight Hospitaller. A bearded pensioner sits by the fire, pipe in mouth. Another figure is seated behind a rough wooden table with tankard at hand, while another stands in his red uniform and round, peaked cap, a uniform similar to that worn by the Chelsea Pensioners. Nell Gwynne is shown with her basket of oranges, although a better representation of this diminutive lady, with her mop of red hair, is the small picture on the adjoining wall. Another figure peers through a window overlooking the restored chapel, and nearby a patient lies ghastly and pale on his truckle bed.

In the stained glass of the chapel and on a stone shield are the Coningsby Arms, with three rabbits or 'conies', a rebus on the name of the founder. Well to the fore is the Maltese Cross, the badge of the Knights Hospitallers, known later as the Knights of Malta.

Herefordshire is one of the cider-producing counties of the West of England and is the home of Bulmer's cider. Adjoining their factory they have a colourful cider museum, illustrating the whole history of cider-making, the various types of cider apples and the different cider presses. Cider was always the main drink of the West Country, Herefordshire, Gloucestershire, Somerset and Devon and, judging by the vast amounts the farmers allowed their labourers, up to a gallon a day in summer, their stamina must have been great. Indeed, to cider was given the credit for long life and health attributed to country folk, although considering the child mortality this might have been due to the survival of the fittest. The unclarified farm-produced cider, 'scrumpy', is now little made. When I first came to the West Country, it was only a few pence a pint, and beer was much dearer. One country pub I knew used to have a saucepan, sugar and ginger by the side of the fire in winter, and when I bought my pint, I would imitate the locals and heat it on the fire, adding sugar and ginger to make a warming, tasty sort of punch. One story told about the farm scrumpy was that it had to be fed lumps of meat to keep it mellow and that if a rat or two got in, they were soon dissolved in the acid liquid. In fact, when I bought a few gallons of cider from a farm, I would feed it with a date or two to keep it from going sour. Another thing about the unclarified scrumpy was that it was always served in a mug and never in a glass because the usually cloudy drink looked better that way. As with most home made beverages, the quality was never uniform, sometimes thin and sharp, sometimes deep yellow and mellow. You never quite know what you were going to get when you asked for scrumpy at a country pub. Commercial ciders have been 'clarified' – cleared of the cloud formed by the residue of apple mash – by means of filters, as many drinkers prefer to see what is in the bottom of their glass. Having spent most of my life in cider country, I prefer my scrumpy, when I can get it, in a raw state served in a handled mug, the best drink to go with a great hunk of bread and a liberal portion of cheese.

After the last war, with more money in their pockets, more countrymen became beer-drinkers, but with the perverse way of fashion, cider became popular among the townspeople, particularly the ladies. The cider factories producing clarified, refined cider with stable qualities of dryness and sweetness flourished. When the tax was raised to something like that on beer, the farm-made product became uneconomic and the price of cider soared, although a few farms still produce the original scrumpy.

The old cider-presses are now used as decorative pieces. I was sitting on the edge of one of these when an old chap got into conversation.

'How did this thing work?' he asked.

'Oh,' I said, 'they just put the apples into the trough and they were squashed by that large stone wheel operated by a horse. The apple juice came out of that spout on the edge of the trough into a vat.'

'Yes,' said the old man thoughtfully, 'but how did they put the "booze" into it?'

Beside cider, Hereford is associated with cattle, for the Hereford cattle with their red coats and white or mottled faces are world famous for their beef quality and adaptability to all variations of climate. Hereford, where much of the stock is sold, is responsible for the ancestry of much of the cattle today on the ranches of America, on the cattle lands of Australia, Argentina, Africa and elsewhere. Perhaps more correctly the credit is due to Lord Scudamore of Holme Lacy, who, in the seventeenth century, brought back from northern France the red stock to mix with his own cattle to produce the first of the Hereford breed. It is a wonder there is no commemorative tablet at Holme Lacy where the breed was originally developed.

There are other museums in Hereford, the city of many museums, including the Bulmer Railway Centre, although perhaps you wonder what the great cider firm has to do with railways: it had to transport its produce, of course, and Bulmer's had a cider train. In 1968 its resting place was provided by the firm to house also the famous *King George V* Great Western Railway locomotive which they had restored. These exhibits attracted other railway enthusiasts who enjoyed the facilities offered by Bulmer's and added some of their own collections,

Hereford Town Hall

including the London Midland & Scottish Railway locomotive *Princess Elizabeth*. Steam open-days are held on occasions.

Another museum likely to attract those interested in engineering is the Herefordshire Waterworks or Broomy Hill Engines Museum in an old pumping station adjoining the Wye. This contains a considerable amount of pumping plant, and apart from working exhibits some of the gauges and pumping equipment can be operated by visitors.

If you are interested in military matters, there is the Regimental Museum with its display of uniforms, medals, weapons and records of battles, but if your tastes are of a more peaceful nature, there is the fascinating Churchill Gardens Museum, with its display of furnishings, costumes, paintings and other items of the late eighteenth and nineteenth centuries.

Before visiting any of the museums, it is as well to check the opening days and times with the City of Hereford Tourist Information Centre in St Owen's Street, as some do not open every day. Hereford has a Guild of Guides who, in the high season, conduct morning and afternoon walks around the City.

So at Hereford, we end our journey up the most spectacular part of the Wye Valley from the lower tidal reaches of the river, through gorges and rapids, cliffs, bog and moorland, through conifer forests and deciduous woodland to quiet water meadows, along the constantly winding road and river, littered with abandoned pools of forgotten industry. On our travels, we have seen something of the wildlife of the valley and have visited the ruined abbey, ancient churches and historic towns, still alive with the bustle of modern life. We have collected a long procession of colourful characters, from Henry Marten at Chepstow to Valentine Morris at Piercefield, from Wintour making his famous leap to John Wesley in the pond at Devauden Green, from the wizard John at Kentchurch to John Kyrle at Ross, from the Mortimers at Hellens to Nell Gwynne at Hereford. I hope you have enjoyed the journey.

Bibliography

Abbeys
Knight, Jeremy, *Tintern and the Romantic Movement* (DoE, 1977)
Robinson, David M., *Tintern Abbey – Official Guide* (Cadw, 1986)

Archaeology
Hart, Cyril, *Archaeology in Dean* (Bellows, 1967)

Beachley
Waters, Ivor, *Beachley* (Army Apprentices' College, Chepstow, 1977)

Castles
Official Guides: Caldicot Castle (Chepstow RDC); Chepstow Castle, Goodrich Castle, Grosmont Castle, Monmouth Castle and Great Castle House, Skenfrith Castle (HMSO)
Perks, J. Clifford, *The Archaeological History of Chepstow Castle during the Middle Ages* (Bristol & Glos. Arch. Soc. Proc., Vol. LXVII, 1946–8)

Chepstow
Farr, Grahame, *Chepstow Ships* (Chepstow Society, 1954)
Lucas, Pat, *Fifty Years of Racing at Chepstow* (H. G. Walters, Tenby, 1976)
Waters, Ivor, *About Chepstow* (Chepstow Society, 1952)
Waters, Ivor, *Piercefield on the banks of the Wye* (F. J. Comber, Chepstow, 1975)

General
Baker, Harry, and Morris, Mike, *The Middle Marches* (Hale, 1983)
Barber, W. T., *West of the Wye* (R. H. Johns, 1965)

Hart, Cyril, *The Verderers and Forest Laws of Dean* (David & Charles, 1971)

Jones, P. Thoresby, *Welsh Border Country* (Batsford, 1946)

Senior, Michael, *Portrait of South Wales* (Hale, 1974)

Various, *A Lower Wye Valley Miscellany* (Lower Wye Valley Preservation Society, 1977)

Geology

Dreghorn, W. *Geology explained in the Forest of Dean and the Wye Valley* (David & Charles, 1968)

George, T. Neville, *British Regional Geology, South Wales* (HMSO, 1970)

Pocock, R. W., and Whitehead, T. W., *British Regional Geology, The Welsh Borderland* (HMSO, 1935)

Gloucestershire

Hutton, Edward, *Highways and Byways of Gloucestershire* (Macmillan, 1936)

Rudder, *History of Gloucestershire* (A. Sutton, 1779)

Verey, David, *Gloucestershire, the Vale and the Forest of Dean* (Edit. Pevsner, Penguin, 1970)

Gwent

Evans, C. J. O., *Monmouthshire, History and Topography* (William Lewis, Cardiff, 1953)

Hando, Fred, J., *Out and About in Monmouthshire* (Johns, Newport, 1958)

Howell, Raymond, *Fedw Villages* (Village Publishing, Cwmbran, 1985)

Phillips, Olive, *Monmouthshire* (Hale, 1951)

Searle, E. J., *The Rivers of Monmouthshire* (1970)

Wade, G. W. and J. H., *Monmouthshire* (Methuen, 1909)

Herefordshire

Bannister, A. T., *The Cathedral Church of Hereford* (1924)

Pevsner, Nikolaus, *Herefordshire* (Penguin, 1963)

Tonkin, J. W., *Herefordshire* (Batsford, 1977)

Metalworking and mining

Jenkins, Rhys, *The Copper Works at Redbrook and Bristol* (Trans. Bristol & Glos. Arch. Soc., Vol. LXIII, 1942)

Nicholls, Rev. H. G., *Iron Making in the Forest of Dean* (1866; republished by Forest Bookshop, Coleford, 1981)

Paar, H. W., *An Industrial Tour of Wye Valley and Forest of Dean* (West London Industrial Archaeological Society, 1980)

The Royal Forest of Dean Free Miners Association (Published by the Royal Forest of Dean Free Miners Association, Secretary, Ray Wright, Cinderford, GL14 2QT, 1974)

Monmouth
Kissack, K., *Monmouth, the Making of a County Town* (Phillimore, 1975)

Offa's Dyke
Wright, C. J., *A Guide to Offa's Dyke Path* (Constable, 1976)

The Wye Valley
Bradley, A. G., *The Wye* (Black, 1910)
Fletcher, H. L. V., *Portrait of the Wye Valley* (Hale, 1968)
Kissack, K., *The River Wye* (Terence Dalton, 1978)
Sale, Richard, *The Wye Valley* (Wildwood House, 1984)
Waters, Ivor, *Inns and Taverns of the Wye Valley* (Chepstow Society, 1976)
The Wye Valley (Ward Lock, 1959)

Ordnance maps
The Wye Valley and Forest of Dean (Outdoor Leisure Map, 1:25000, Ordnance Survey)
Gloucester and Forest of Dean (1:50,000, Sheet 162, Ordnance Survey)
Hereford and Leominster (1:50,000, Sheet 149, Ordnance Survey)

Index